SUCCESSFUL INDOOR GARDENING
EXOTIC
FOLIAGE
HOUSEPLANTS

William Davidson

HPBooks
a division of
PRICE STERN SLOAN
Los Angeles

A Salamander Book

© 1989 by Salamander Books Ltd.,
52 Bedford Row, London WC1R 4LR,
United Kingdom.

Published by HPBooks, a division of Price Stern Sloan, Inc.
360 North La Cienega Boulevard, Los Angeles, California 90048.
Printed in Belgium.

9 8 7 6 5 4 3 2 1

All rights reserved. No part of this publication may be reproduced, stored in a retrieval system or transmitted, in any form or by any means, electronic, mechanical, photocopying, recording or otherwise, without the prior written permission of the publisher.

This book may not be sold outside the United States of America or Canada.

Library of Congress Cataloging-in-Publication Data

Davidson, William.
    Exotic foliage houseplants / by William Davidson.
      p. cm. – – (Successful indoor gardening)
    Includes index.
    ISBN 0-89586-834-2 $9.95 ($12.95 Can.)
    1. House plants.   2. Foliage plants.   I. Title.   II. Series.
SB419.D3675   1989
635.9'65 – – dc19
                                              89-1982
                                                CIP

Credits

Introduction written by: David Squire
Editor: Geoffrey Rogers
Assistant editor: Lisa Dyer
Designer: Suzie Baker
Photographer: Eric Crichton
Line artwork: Tyler/Camoccio Design Consultants
Typeset by: Gee Graphics Ltd.
Color separation by: Magnum Graphics Ltd.
Printed by: Proost International Book Production, Turnhout, Belgium

Contents

Introduction	6
Easy to Grow	14
Moderately Easy to Grow	30
Difficult to Grow	70
Index	95

INTRODUCTION

Introduction

The range of foliage houseplants is much wider than with flowering types, and more appear to be offered for sale each year. Packed with over 75 sumptuous colour photographs, this informative guide features many of the more exotic varieties, from the ever popular Swiss cheese plant (*Monstera deliciosa*) to the fascinating Venus's flytrap (*Dionaea muscipula*). The plants are grouped according to the ease with which they can be cultivated, and detailed growing instructions include such essential information as the water, light and temperature requirements of each species.

Many of the plants do not need high temperatures, even in winter. Others, including the large-leaved and decorous philodendrons and the eye-catching peacock plant (*Calathea makoyana*), need warmth. Their need for light also varies, from those plants such as *Yucca aloifolia* which prefers good light, to philodendrons which need slight shade if the leaves are not to be damaged.

Buying foliage houseplants
Select your houseplants with care: poor specimens do not develop properly and the problem usually gets worse until eventually the plant has to be discarded. To ensure success, follow these simple guidelines when buying foliage houseplants.
- Always buy plants from reputable sources.
- Don't buy plants which are displayed outside shops, especially in winter. The foliage becomes chilled, encouraging leaves to fall off or wind-burned areas to appear around the leaf edges. Also, in summer the compost becomes dry and causes wilting, especially of soft-leaved plants.
- Don't buy plants infested with pests or diseases. Not only will the plant be marred but it will infect other plants when you get it home.
- Don't buy plants with roots growing out of drainage holes. Also, avoid plants with algae or slime on the compost or pot.

Above: This group of codiaeums, dieffenbachias, sansevierias and Swiss cheese plants show the wide range of foliage plants available.

Right: Greenhouses offer an ideal environment for houseplants, providing plenty of room for plants to grow to their full size.

Buying Foliage Houseplants

- Avoid plants with dry or excessively wet compost.
- Don't buy plants which are not labelled. It becomes a continuing annoyance if you cannot tell friends the plant's name.
- Don't buy plants with wilting leaves.
- Don't buy a plant which has only recently been repotted as it will not be fully anchored in its pot.
- Avoid foliage plants which are obviously in too small pots. Their roots will have become constricted and even if rapidly repotted a plant may not recover. Also, large foliage plants in small pots are soon knocked over and damaged.

Getting foliage plants home
Equally important as selecting and buying the right plant is getting your plant home safely. Here are a few clues to success.
- Make buying foliage plants the last job on your shopping list: there is then less chance of them being damaged. This is especially important when buying large plants.
- Avoid putting foliage houseplants in cold or excessively hot car boots (trunks). In temperature extremes, place the plants in a box inside the car, but safe from the ravages of young children or dogs.
- Ask for the plant to be wrapped in a plastic or paper sleeve, especially in winter when cold wind soon damages the foliage.
- Get your plant home quickly, especially in winter.

Acclimatizing new plants
Once you have got your new plant home you should quickly establish it as follows:
- Remove the plant from the wrapping as soon as you get home. Take care when removing a tight-fitting sleeve – it is best just to slit the sleeve down the side, rather than to slip the plant out of it.
- Place your plant in moderate shade and warmth, away from draughts. After about ten days, move the plant to its permanent position. During this period, some plants may drop a few leaves, but as long as this is in moderation, the plant will not suffer.
- Ensure that the compost is moist, but not totally saturated.
- Avoid knocking plants, and do not keep moving them around a room in order to find the best position. It is well worth taking the time to acclimatize your plant to its new surroundings.

INTRODUCTION

Getting the Best from Foliage Houseplants

The pleasure you get from foliage houseplants – and the time they remain attractive - greatly depends on the way you care for them. Foliage plants do not react to neglect so rapidly as flowering houseplants, but long-term damage can often be done by providing the wrong conditions. Here are a few ways to help you get the best from your plants.

Watering All foliage plants are individual and the frequency and amount of water they need varies enormously. Some like to have their roots continually wet, but most plants need to have the compost kept moist but not saturated. In practice, it is best to saturate the compost and then to wait until it is showing signs of becoming dry before applying more water.

Some plants dislike lime in the compost, as well as in the water you give them. If your water is hard and limy, use water which has been boiled and allowed to cool. Alternatively, and if the water is only slightly alkaline, run the water for several minutes before collecting it in a watering-can; allow it to stand and settle before use. Most plants, however, live quite happily for years on tap water and it is only if you have a sensitive plant that you need to take care.

Feeding By the time a plant is bought, it is likely to need further applications of fertilizer. This is because when a plant is potted the nutrients in the compost last the plant six to eight weeks and by the time it is sold these have often become exhausted. Fertilizers can be applied in several ways: as a concentrated liquid added to water; as granules applied to the surface of the compost; or as pills or sticks of fertilizers pressed into the compost. For many people, the liquid form is still the best method as it can easily be withheld during the winter months when the plant is not growing rapidly.

Foliage plants usually live for many years and it is vital that during this time they do not become starved and their growth checked. Plants should be fed only when they are growing strongly, which usually means between mid spring and late autumn. However, if plants are grown under special growth-promoting lights, feeding can continue. Normally, foliage houseplants should be fed every two to three weeks, although in some cases this may be more frequent – see specific instructions for individual species.

Mist spraying Plants from tropical and sub-tropical regions especially benefit from a relatively humid atmosphere. This is mainly achieved by using a mist-sprayer to cover the leaf surfaces with small droplets of water. However, do not do this to plants with soft and hairy leaves as it encourages them to rot. During the height of summer, plants can be sprayed several times a day, but this should not be carried out too late in the day as all moisture should have dried before nightfall. Moisture which remains on leaves and in leaf joints at night, when the temperature falls, encourages the onset of diseases.

Temperature The temperature in which a houseplant is placed plays an important role in both the plant's long- and short-term health. To help you decide where best to keep a plant, the ideal temperature range has been indicated for each species. If the ideal temperature cannot be achieved – which is often the case at night during the winter, when the central heating has been turned down or off – you should keep the compost slightly drier than usual.

Getting the Best from Foliage Houseplants

Grooming Because it is the leaves of foliage plants which are the chief attraction, it is important that they are kept bright and in good condition. Large leaves benefit from being regularly cleaned by wiping them with a damp cloth.

Proprietary leaf-cleaning solutions can be used, as well as milk, but usually water alone is best. Don't leave smears on the leaves and take care not to leave the surfaces wet and the plant in strong, direct sunlight. When small water globules are left on leaves they act like lenses in full sunlight and cause the surface to be burned. Hairy-leaved plants are best cleaned with a soft brush.

Compost Newly-bought foliage houseplants will probably last out the season in the same compost, but during the following spring they may need to be repotted. Plants should only be repotted when the compost is full of roots. Foliage houseplants, especially large ones, are more commonly grown in loam-based composts than peat-based ones, because loam creates a heavier and more secure base than peat. Small foliage plants are ideal in peat-based composts.

Above: It is important to give your foliage houseplants the correct conditions. Nephthytis podophyllum needs particular attention if it is to flourish, requiring warmth, moisture and shade.

INTRODUCTION

Displaying Foliage Houseplants

The range of foliage houseplants is wide, with types to suit every part of your home. Some plants are upright, large and dominant, others small and ideal for even the smallest of table displays. Here are a few ideas on using them.

Table-top displays Tables of all kinds make ideal homes for foliage plants. Round and oval tables are best decorated with plants displaying an even outline. Bear in mind that plants placed on a dining table are viewed mainly from the side and therefore require a good side-on 'face'. Plants placed on low coffee tables, on the other hand, are usually seen from above and need to have a shorter and relatively wider stance, with the leaves forming a slightly more horizontal attitude.

Group displays Small foliage houseplants are frequently sold in decorative groups planted in a small, shallow bowl up to 25cm (10in) long. These include small palms, such as *Chamaedorea elegans*, the

Above: A group of houseplants always creates interest, especially when displayed in an attractive container. A range of contrasting shapes and colours, such as seen here, makes an attractive display that will last and draw attention for several months.

Displaying Foliage Houseplants

polka dot plant (*Hypoestes sanguinolenta*), and the aluminium plant (*Pilea cadierei nana*), as well as small ferns. Invariably, the display remains attractive for a few weeks, then one plant starts to dominate the arrangement. The plants are then best repotted individually.

Small plants growing in their own individual pots can also be grouped together. This method of grouping means the display can easily be re-arranged. The individual pots can be placed in a large and attractive outer container, with moist peat packed between them to keep the compost moist and help to create more humidity.

Groups of plants can also be used to create floor-standing arrangements, either in well-lit corners or by the sides of patio windows. These are usually formed of one large and dominant foliage plant with an array of foliage and flowering plants around the base. To prevent the carpet or floor becoming damaged, stand these plants in individual saucers or on one large tray.

Indoor hanging baskets These are similar to outdoor hanging baskets but have built into them a drip tray or the space for a plastic saucer in which the flower pot can stand. Both trailing and cascading foliage plants can be displayed in hanging baskets. Plants to look for include *Pellionia daveauana*, hearts entangled (*Ceropegia woodii*), the velvet plant (*Gynura sarmentosa*) and snakeskin plants (*Fittonias*).

Displays in troughs Troughs, with a range of upright foliage plants as well as cascading and trailing plants around the edges to soften the outline, create an attractive feature. Leave the plants in their individual pots and pack moist peat around them.

Illuminating plants Large-leaved foliage plants, such as the Swiss cheese plant (*Monstera deliciosa*) and some of the large-leaved philodendrons, look especially attractive when highlighted with a spot light, especially in winter and if the plant is in a relatively dull position. However, the quality of light emitted by a tungsten-filament bulb is not the type that encourages plants to grow, and if placed too close to the foliage it may cause burns. Nonetheless, a spotlight does make an attractive feature and, if used in combination with dimmed room lights, the result can be eye-catching.

The use of mirrors A large foliage plant positioned in an alcove, with a full-length mirror behind it, creates a stunningly attractive feature. You can accentuate the effect by using a spotlight to highlight the plant.

Displays in alcoves Any large recess in a wall, especially if it is arched and the wall is white or light-coloured, provides a superb background feature for palms and other large-leaved foliage plants. The paradise palm *Howeia forsteriana* is ideal for large alcoves. This palm can also be advantageously positioned either side of a door. In small recesses, you can use either indoor hanging baskets or wall-brackets to introduce an attractive display of trailing plants.

Cache pots These attractive outer pots are ideal for enhancing clay or plastic pots which lack eye-appeal, and they can be chosen to harmonize with the foliage. They are usually ornate and attractively coloured plastic, but can be pottery or ornate metals such as copper.

Take care when using cache pots that they do not become full of stagnant water as this will keep the compost too wet and cold, and cause the roots to rot.

INTRODUCTION

Plants as camouflage Few homes are without a feature which is in need of camouflage, whether it is central-heating pipes, surface-laid electricity wires or cold water or gas pipes. Plants can be used either to camouflage the unsightly feature or to draw attention away from it. Highlighting plants with mirrors or lights takes the eye away, but if you want to camouflage the feature try a climbing plant positioned in front of it. Climbing foliage houseplants include the begonia vine (*Cissus discolor*), the Swiss cheese plant (*Monstera deliciosa*) and elephant's ear (*Philodendron hastatum*), but always ensure that the foliage does not touch heating or hot water pipes as this will cause it to wilt.

Good Health Guide

There are three main problems which flowering houseplants are likely to encounter: pests which eat the leaves, stems and roots; diseases which can soon create an unsightly mess; and physiological disorders which result from poor conditions.

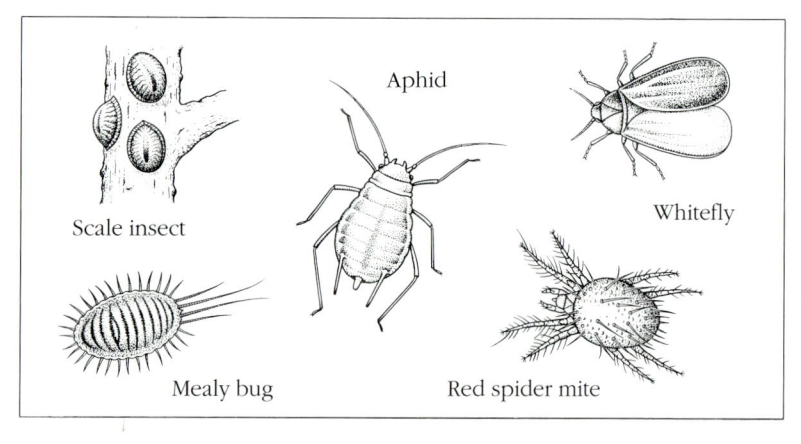

Above: These are some of the pests that may attack your houseplants. To eradicate them, spray infested plants with pesticide.

Below: Here mealy bugs cluster on the leaves of a codiaeum. They soon disfigure plants, so use an insecticide immediately.

Good Health Guide

Plant infesting pests
- **Aphids**, frequently known as greenfly, are plumpish green insects with or without wings. They cluster around shoot tips, in leaf joints and under soft leaves. They suck sap, weaken the plant and emit a sticky honeydew which encourages black sooty mould to infest the plant. To kill these pests, spray infested plants with an insecticide, repeating the application every 10-14 days.
- **Whitefly** are tiny, rather triangular white flies which cluster mainly on the undersides of soft leaves. Their larvae also mainly cluster on the undersides of leaves, leaving a sticky deposit which encourages the presence of sooty mould. To kill these pests, spray in the same way as for aphids.
- **Red spider mites** are minute, red, brownish-red or straw-coloured 'spiders' which infest houseplants, especially when the air is dry and the temperature high. Leaves assume yellow mottling and webbing may also occur. Mist-spray the leaves regularly, as this prevents an attack building up to epidemic proportions. Also, regularly spray infected plants with a systemic insecticide.
- **Mealy bugs** are slow-moving – eventually static – pests which resemble small and woolly woodlice. They usually cluster beneath leaves and in leaf joints. Light infestations can be controlled by wiping them away with a damp cotton bud. Severely infested plants, however, will need to be sprayed regularly with an insecticide.
- **Scale insects** are hard, brownish, static discs which usually cluster on the undersides of leaves and along stems. They are unsightly and severe infestations cause leaves to become yellow. Light infestations of scale insects can be controlled with moist cotton buds, but established colonies are difficult to eradicate and repeated sprayings with an insecticide are necessary.

Plant diseases
- **Botrytis**, also known as grey mould, forms a grey, fluffy mould which can cover all the plant, especially if it is soft. Poor ventilation and still and cool conditions encourage its presence. Cut away badly infected parts and destroy the plant if it becomes totally infected. Spraying with a fungicide helps both to prevent and control this disease.
- **Sooty mould** is a black fungus which grows on the sticky excretions of aphids, whiteflies, scale insects and mealy bugs. Leaves become covered with a black, powdery deposit. Wipe off the mould with a damp cloth, then rinse the plant with clean water. Spray regularly with a pesticide to control the sucking pests which cause this disease.
- **Powdery mildew** creates a disfiguring white, powdery coating or white fluffy growth on leaves. It may eventually attack flowers and stems. Remove and burn severely infected leaves and spray the rest of the plant with a fungicide.

Physiological disorders
These occur because a plant has not been given the correct treatment. Here are a couple of the problems which can arise.
- **Wilting** happens mainly when the compost is kept too dry, but water-saturated compost also causes wilting. If the compost is dry, add water; if too wet, remove the soil-ball and allow it to partly dry before returning it to the pot.
- **Sun scald**, in the form of brown, papery patches, occurs on leaves and flowers which have been misted and then positioned in strong sunlight.

EASY

Easy to Grow

Foliage houseplants form the permanent part of any collection of plants within the home. They retain their foliage throughout the year and display a wonderful array of green or variegated leaves in a wide range of shapes and sizes. Luckily, the most attractive varieties of foliage plant are not necessarily the most difficult to grow. The plants in this section are all easy to care for, demanding little attention and surviving low temperatures during the winter, yet amongst them are some of the most attractive of all foliage houseplants. The colourful rex begonia (*Begonia rex*), the striking mother-in-law's tongue (*Sansevieria trifasciata*) and the stately boundary plant (*Yucca aloifolia*) are all eye-catching species which are easily established and cared for in the home.

Abutilon

Abutilon sevitzia
(Abutilon hybridum 'Sevitzia')
CHINESE LANTERN
FLOWERING MAPLE

Vigorous growing plant for cooler conditions that offer good light, but not full sun when close to glass. Has attractively variegated maple-type leaves and pendulous orange-coloured flowers not unlike a small single hollyhock.

A loam-based mixture is essential when potting plants on – a task that must not be neglected if plants are to do as well as they can. While in active growth feed at every watering, to keep colour. Firm cuttings about 10cm (4in) in length will root readily in peaty mixture if placed in a heated propagator; when growth begins, remove the growing tip of the cutting. When well cared for, individual stems will put on 90cm (3ft) of growth in one season, but pruning can be undertaken at any time to limit growth. Never allow plants to stand in water for long periods, but water copiously while fresh leaves appear.

Soft growth attracts many pests, so a careful and frequent check is advised, especially under the leaves.

Take care
Whitefly can be a nuisance.

☐ Good light
☐ Temp: 13-18°C (55-65°F)
☐ Frequent feeding

Left: Abutilon sevitzia is a colourful, free-growing plant that thrives in moderate temperatures and good lighting. You may prune it to desired shape and size at any time.

EASY

Above: Distinctive brown markings in the centre of the leaf give Begonia masoniana the apt common name of 'iron cross begonia'. Plants develop into neat, rounded shapes as they age. This plant has rough textured foliage which makes cleaning impossible other than by dusting with a soft brush.

Begonia masoniana
IRON CROSS BEGONIA

This fine plant grows to splendid size if given reasonable care. The rough-surfaced leaves are a brownish green in colour and have a very distinctive cross that covers the greater part of the centre of the leaf and radiates from the area where the petiole is joined. This marking resembles the German Iron Cross.

During the spring and summer months it will be found that plants grow at a reasonable pace if given a warm room, moist root conditions, and weak liquid fertilizer with each watering. Plants that have filled their existing pots with roots can be potted on at any time during the summer, using a loam-based potting mixture and shallow pots. Over the winter months loss of some lower leaves will be almost inevitable, but provided the soil is kept on the dry side during this time the plant will remain in better condition and will grow away with fresh leaves in the spring.

Take care
Inspect for winter rot.

- Light shade
- Temp: 16-21°C (60-70°F)
- Keep dry in winter

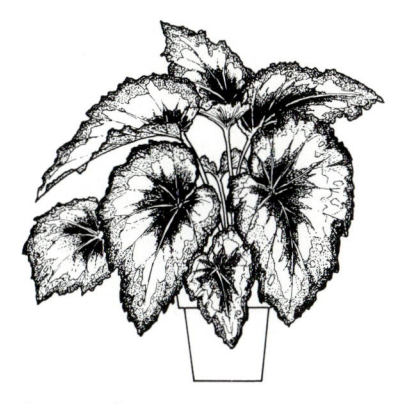

Begonia

Begonia rex
PAINTED LEAF BEGONIA
REX BEGONIA

These rank among the finest foliage plants, with all shades of colouring and intricate leaf patterns. Those with smaller leaves are generally easier to care for indoors.

To propagate, firm, mature leaves are removed from the plant and most of the leaf stalk is removed before a series of cuts are made through the thick veins on the underside of the leaf. The leaf is then placed underside down on moist peat (in either boxes or shallow pans) and a few pebbles are placed on top of the leaf, to keep it in contact with the moist peat. Temperatures in the region of 21°C (70°F) are required, and a propagating case.

Alternatively, the leaf can be cut into squares of about 5cm (2in), and the pieces placed on moist peat.

When purchased these plants are often in pots that are much too small; repot the plant into a larger container without delay, using peaty compost.

Take care
In close conditions look out for signs of mildew developing.

- Light shade
- Temp: 16-21°C (60-70°F)
- Keep on the dry side in winter

Below: A wealth of colour in the foliage and intricate leaf patterns place Begonia rex among the elite of houseplants. These plants vary in their ease of culture, with smaller-leaved, more compact types being generally easier to raise. The plant's leaves are borne on stems which grow from the rhizome.

EASY

Grevillea robusta
SILK OAK
SILKY OAK

An Australian plant, the silk oak makes a splendid tree in its native land, and is a fairly fast-growing pot plant in many other parts of the world. It is tough, has attractive, green silky foliage and is one of the easiest plants to care for. It can be readily raised from seed.

The grevillea will quickly grow into a large plant if it is kept moist and well fed, and if it is potted into a larger container when the existing one is well filled with roots. A loam-based soil is best. If plants become too tall for their allotted space it is no trouble to remove the more invasive branches with a pair of secateurs – almost any time of the year will do for this exercise.

During the summer months when the plant is in full vigour it will be important to ensure that it is obtaining sufficient water, and this will mean filling the top of the pot and ensuring that the surplus runs right through and out at the bottom drainage holes.

Take care
Water well in summer.

☐ Good light
☐ Temp: 4-7°C (40-45°F)
☐ Feed and water well

Iresine

Below left: When well grown, the leaves of Grevillea robusta have a silvery sheen that is most attractive. The 'silk oak' needs cool and light conditions.

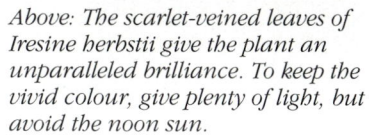

Above: The scarlet-veined leaves of Iresine herbstii give the plant an unparalleled brilliance. To keep the vivid colour, give plenty of light, but avoid the noon sun.

Iresine herbstii
BEEFSTEAK PLANT
BLOOD LEAF
CHICKEN GIZZARD

These fall among the cheap and cheerful range of plants, and have foliage of a very deep, almost unnatural red. Cuttings root very easily and plants are quick to grow; they can be propagated successfully on the windowsill if shaded from direct sun.

Mature plants, however, must have a very light place if they are to retain their colouring, and will only need protection from strong midday sun. During the spring and summer plants must be kept active by regular feeding and ensuring that the soil does not dry out excessively. When potting on becomes necessary a loam-based mixture should be used; plants will soon use the nourishment in peat mixes even if fed regularly. At all stages of growth the appearance of the plant will be improved if the tips are periodically removed.

Besides the red-coloured variety there is *I. herbstii aureoreticulata*, which has yellow colouring and needs the same attention.

Take care
Feed well in summer.

- ☐ Good light
- ☐ Temp: 13-18°C (55-65°F)
- ☐ Keep fed and watered

EASY

Mimosa pudica
HUMBLE PLANT
LIVE-AND-DIE
SENSITIVE PLANT
SHAME PLANT
TOUCH-ME-NOT

These are attractive little plants with fern-like foliage, which are grown as annuals, fresh seed being sown each spring and old plants discarded at the end of the summer. The main attraction of this plant lies in its habit of collapsing completely during the day when the foliage is touched. In time the plant becomes erect again, but it is an eerie sight.

These plants are frequently offered for sale in very small pots that have

Pellionia

little nutrient left in the soil. Repot into standard houseplant mixture as soon as possible to get a more vigorous plant.

Actively growing plants should be kept moist and fed regularly. Freshly potted plants should be allowed to establish in new soil before being fed. A position in light shade is suggested, but plants will tolerate some sunlight if not too bright.

Take care
Pot on to avoid starvation.

- Light shade
- Temp: 16-21°C (60-70°F)
- Keep moist and fed

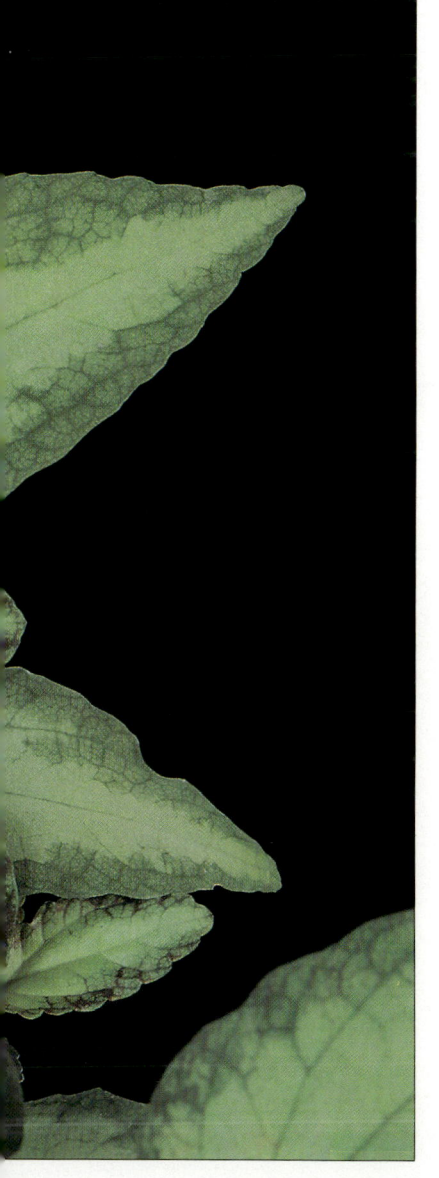

Pellionia daveauana
TRAILING WATERMELON BEGONIA

Very easy plants to care for, and easy to propagate, yet they never seem to make the grade as indoor plants. This is rather odd, as they adapt very well as hanging plants, or do well as a creeper, in the bottle garden, or simply as an addition to the windowsill collection. Leaves are oval-shaped and produced in quantity, and they have an interesting colouring of brown and dull yellow.

To propagate new plants, remove pieces of stem, any section, about 7.5cm (3in) long, and put four or five of these in small pots of peaty houseplant soil. Cuttings can go direct into hanging pots or small baskets if desired. When they get under way, remove the tips to encourage the plant to branch out. It is essential that plants be kept moist and warm, and out of direct sunlight. When potting on becomes necessary one of the many peaty houseplant potting mixtures will suit them fine, but avoid using very large pots.

Take care
Renew older plants periodically.

- Light shade
- Temp: 13-21°C (55-70°F)
- Keep moist and fed

Left: Pellionia daveauana is a naturally hanging or creeping plant with leaves that are about 5cm (2in) in length and multi-coloured. It is easily propagated.

EASY

Above: The glossy green leaves of Philodendron hastatum are broad and arrow-shaped. Plants attain stately proportions in time, even up to 6m (20ft), but they need a supporting structure.

Philodendron hastatum
ELEPHANT'S EAR

Again we have a touch of majesty from the splendid Araceae family of plants, and the common name immediately gives the game away that this is a rather large plant. The leaves are broadly arrow-shaped, glossy green and attached to

Pilea

very bold, tall-growing stems; in a greenhouse it may reach a height of 6m (20ft). Normally indoor growth is thinner and less robust, but the fact that the plant has a tough constitution makes it a reasonably trouble-free plant in agreeable conditions.

As a young plant it will trail, but it is much too important for this style of growing and when purchasing one you should also acquire a moss-covered support (preferably one that can be extended) to which the plant can be tied. If the moss is kept moist by regular spraying with water from a mister it will be found that in time the natural aerial roots of the plant will grow around and into the moss. Leaves can be occasionally wiped with a damp cloth to clean them.

Take care
Avoid dry and sunny positions.

- Shade
- Temp: 16-21°C (60-70°F)
- Keep moist and fed

Pilea cadierei nana
ALUMINIUM PLANT
WATERMELON PILEA

With silvered foliage, this is by far the most popular of the pileas, but there are numerous others, all needing similar treatment.

Plants are started from cuttings taken at any time of the year if temperatures of around 18°C (65°F) and moist, close conditions can be provided. A simple propagating case on the windowsill can offer just these conditions. Top cuttings with four to six leaves are taken, the bottom pair is removed and the end of the stem is treated with rooting powder before up to seven cuttings are inserted in each small pot filled with a peaty mixture. Once cuttings have got under way the growing tips are removed and the plants are potted on into slightly larger containers in loam-based mixture.

Plants should have ample light, but not be exposed to bright sunlight. Although small, pileas need ample feeding during the growing months, if they are to retain their bright colouring.

Take care
Pinch out tips to retain shape.

- Light shade
- Temp: 16-21°C (60-70°F)
- Keep moist and fed

Left: The foliage of Pilea cadierei nana, the 'aluminium plant', is generously speckled with silver. Regular pinching out of the growing tips will produce plants of neat appearance.

EASY

Pleomele reflexa variegata
(Dracaena reflexa variegata)
SONG OF INDIA

These painfully slow-growing plants are not often available: anyone seeing a priced plant should stake a claim immediately! When mature and well grown, this is a fine plant. Stems are very woody, and leaves are miniature but bright yellow. Plants may be no more than 1.5-1.8m (5-6ft) tall, though at least 20 years old. Slow growth is one reason for their scarcity, and for the high price should any be on offer.

Plants enjoy good light, with shade from strong sunlight, and temperatures that fluctuate from 16 to 21°C (60 to 70°F). Water well when necessary, and allow to dry appreciably before watering again, but the surrounding area should be kept moist at all times. Feeding should be done on average once a week in summer, with none at all from the onset of winter to the early spring when new growth appears.

Few pests bother these fine plants, whose worst enemy is a combination of wetness and cold.

Take care
Ensure soil drains freely.

- ☐ Good light
- ☐ Temp: 16-21°C (60-70°F)
- ☐ Keep on dry side

Below: Commonly named 'song of India', Pleomele reflexa variegata is an aristocrat among potted plants. The foliage is almost entirely yellow, with narrow leaves about 15cm (6in) long.

Above right: Pteris cretica albolineata is an attractive fern with pale green and off-white variegation. It needs moist and warm shaded conditions. Bright sun and dry air cause scorching.

Pteris

Pteris cretica albo-lineata
VARIEGATED CRETAN BRAKE
VARIEGATED TABLE FERN

The variegated form of *P. cretica* has a pale green outer margin to its leaves and a cream-coloured central area. There are several other variegated forms available, and all will respond well to shaded and warm conditions where a reasonable degree of humidity can be maintained. They will also benefit from regular feeding once they have become established in their pots. Many of these smaller ferns do very well if fed with a foliar feed, which is sprayed onto the leaves.

Fern plants do very much better if they can be grouped together. Large plastic trays are easily obtainable, and these are ideal for placing groups of ferns and other types of indoor plants. The tray is filled with gravel and well watered before the plants are placed on the surface; it is important that the plant pot base should not stand in water, as this would make the soil much too wet. The wet tray will provide a continual source of essential humidity.

Take care
Never subject ferns to direct sun.

- Shade
- Temp: 16-21°C (60-70°F)
- Keep moist

25

EASY

Sansevieria trifasciata 'Laurentii'
BOWSTRING HEMP
DEVIL'S TONGUE
GOOD-LUCK PLANT
MOTHER-IN-LAW'S TONGUE
SNAKE PLANT

This plant is almost indestructible. The leaves are about 60cm (2ft) long, thick and fleshy, holding a lot of moisture which the plant can draw on as needed; in view of this, it is important not to overwater, nor to give any more than the plant needs.

A good watering once each month in summer should suffice, with none at all during the winter months. This may seem harsh, but if plants are to be exposed to colder winter temperatures they will get through much better if the soil in the pot is dry rather than wet. Potting ought not to be done too frequently, and one can leave the plant until it actually breaks the pot in which it is growing – the swelling bases of leaves within the pot are quite capable of breaking clay as well as plastic pots. Loam-based soil is essential when potting on, and clay pots will help to maintain the balance of these top-heavy plants.

Take care
Avoid cold and wetness together.

- ☐ Good light
- ☐ Temp: 16-21°C (60-70°F)
- ☐ Keep dry

Setcreasea

Setcreasea purpurea
PURPLE HEART

The humble tradescantia has many interesting relatives, including *S. purpurea*. Brilliant purple leaves are seen at their best when the plant is growing in good light with some direct sun, but very strong sun should be guarded against. They are impressive when grown in hanging pots or baskets: with all hanging plants one should endeavour to achieve a full effect, so lots of cuttings should go into each pot.

Cuttings of pieces of stem some 10cm (4in) long will not be hard to root in conventional houseplant potting mixture. Enclosing the cuttings in a small propagator, or even a sealed polythene bag, will reduce transpiration and speed up the rooting process. Several cuttings, up to five in each 7.5cm (3in) pot, will provide better plants than single pieces in the pot.

Like most of the tradescantia tribe, this one should be well watered and allowed to dry appreciably before watering again. Feed occasionally.

Take care
Replace old plants by cuttings.

- Good light
- Temp: 10-16°C (50-60°F)
- Avoid wet conditions

Left: Sansevieria trifasciata 'Laurentii' has bright yellow margins to the leaves, with mottled variegation in the central areas. These plants tolerate direct sunlight and can be very durable if not overwatered.

Below: The leaves of Setcreasea purpurea are purple all over and attached to firm succulent stems. The colour develops most effectively when the plant is in good light. This plant is a member of the tradescantia tribe.

EASY

Stenotaphrum secundatum
BUFFALO GRASS
ST AUGUSTINE'S GRASS

This amazingly invasive grass bounds away in all directions once it has established a foothold. It is not unattractive, with cream and green variegation, the cream being predominant. Its major drawback is that as the plant produces fresh growth, so the older growth shrivels and dies, leaving dry brown leaves hanging from the lower parts of the plant. However, if one has time to remove these as they appear, the plant can be kept looking attractive.

Tufts of grassy leaves with a thicker base are produced in profusion; any removed and pushed into pots of peaty soil root almost at once. When plants appear to be past their best, root fresh cuttings and dispose of the aged parent. This is best done in the autumn, so that one will have more manageable plants to care for over the winter.

These plants will grow anywhere if there is moisture and warmth, and are very welcome as something different in the way of hanging plants.

Take care
Renew older plants regularly.

- Light shade
- Temp: 10-16°C (50-60°F)
- Keep very moist and fed

Yucca aloifolia
BOUNDARY PLANT
DAGGER PLANT
SPANISH BAYONET

The woody lengths of stem are imported from the tropics in very large quantities; they come in an assortment of sizes and are rooted at their destination, then potted and sold with their attractive aloe-like tufts of growth at the top of the stem.

Yucca

Further benefits of this plant are that they are pleasing to the eye when grouped together, and little trouble to grow.

They do best in well-lit, coolish rooms if given the minimum of attention. The soil should be allowed to dry out quite appreciably between waterings and feed should be given once every 10 days during the summer months.

Purchased plants are normally in pots relevant to their height, so the pot is often quite large; as a result of this, the plant is growing in a container in which it can remain for two years or more. Plants should be potted only when they have well filled their existing pots with roots. Use loam-based soil for this job when it is done.

Take care
Never overpot or overwater.

- Good light
- Temp: 10-21°C (50-70°F)
- Keep on the dry side

Above: Amazingly vigorous plants, Stenotaphrum secundatum will quickly fill their allotted space. They are effective in hanging baskets, where the narrow variegated leaves can easily be seen.

Below: Yucca aloifolia is a stately plant for difficult locations as it is very durable if not overwatered. These plants are normally seen as stout stems with tufts of growth at the top.

MODERATE

Moderately Easy to Grow

The plants features in this section should create few problems for houseplant enthusiasts, though they do require special care if they are to remain attractive for a long time. They range from the stately palms *Howeia forsteriana* and *Phoenix canariensis* to the eye-catching earth stars (*Cryptanthus*) and the exotic ivory pineapple (*Ananas bracteatus striatus*).

Many of the plants require conditions that are warm and humid; some also need careful watering during the winter months. Advice on how to water individual plants is provided for each species – but do remember that the amount of water a plant requires is related to the plant's size, the temperature, the amount of natural light the plant is receiving and the time of year.

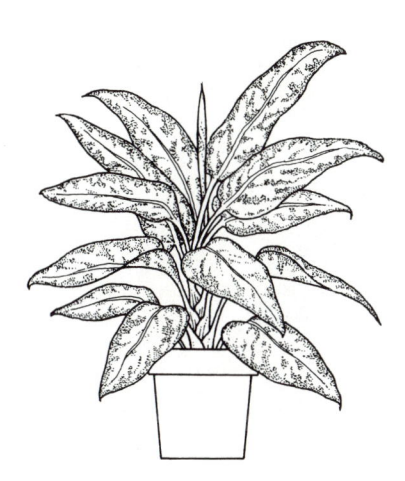

Aglaonema

Aglaonema crispum 'Silver Queen'
CHINESE EVERGREEN
SILVER SPEAR

There are numerous aglaonemas that form central clumps that increase in size as plants mature, but the variety A. 'Silver Queen' is superior in all respects. Individual spear-shaped leaves are produced at soil level and have a grey-green background colouring liberally spotted with silver.

New plants are made by separating the clumps at any time of year and potting them individually in a peaty mixture in small pots. As plants mature they can be potted on into slightly larger containers, and will in time produce offsets of their own. For the second and subsequent potting operations, use a potting mix that contains some loam, but it should still be very much on the peaty side. Warm, moist and shaded conditions are essential if leaves are to retain their texture and brightness. Watering requires some care; plants must be moist at all times, but not saturated, especially in winter.

Take care
Mealy bug can weaken growth.

- ☐ Light shade
- ☐ Temp: 18-21°C (65-70°F)
- ☐ Keep moist

Left: A member of the Araceae family, Aglaonema crispum 'Silver Queen' thrives in warm, moist and shady conditions.

Aglaonema pseudobracteatum
CHINESE EVERGREEN
GOLDEN EVERGREEN

A demanding plant, best suited to the experienced grower; the principal difficulty is the high temperature, which must be maintained. A height of 1m (39in) is not unusual in mature specimens. Leaf perimeter is green with a centre of whitish yellow.

New plants are propagated from top sections of stems with three sound leaves attached. Severed ends are allowed to dry for a few hours before being treated with rooting powder; plant in peaty mixture in small pots, and plunge in moist peat in a heated propagating case; to ensure success the temperature should be around 21°C (70°F). When potting cuttings for growing on, put three cuttings in a 13cm (5in) pot, using a potting mixture with a percentage of loam.

These plants are not much troubled by pests, but mealy bugs are sometimes found where the leaf stalks curl round the main stem. In this situation, thorough saturation with liquid insecticide will be needed.

Take care
Ensure adequate temperature.

- ☐ Light shade
- ☐ Temp: 18-21°C (65-70°F)
- ☐ Keep moist

MODERATE

Ananas bracteatus striatus
IVORY PINEAPPLE

The best of the South American bromeliads, the green form of which, *A. comosus*, is the pineapple of commerce. A white variegated form of *A. comosus* is also known as the ivory pineapple.

In good light the natural cream colouring of the foliage will be a much better colour, but one should avoid very strong sunlight that is magnified by clear glass. Wet root conditions that offer little drying out will also be harmful. Feed occasionally but avoid overdoing it. New plants can be produced by pulling offsets from mature plants and potting them individually in a mixture containing leaf mould and peat. In reasonable conditions plants can be expected to develop small pineapples in about five years; although highly decorative, these tend to be woody and inedible. However, as pineapples are developing, the central part of the plant around the base of the leaves will change to a brilliant reddish pink.

Take care
Avoid the spined leaf margins.

- Good light
- Temp: 13-18°C (55-65°F)
- Keep on dry side

Above: An extremely ornamental member of the South American bromeliad family, Ananas bracteatus striatus will develop dazzling colour in good light.

Right: Beaucarnea recurvata is a species best displayed as an individual plant. It is tolerant of a wide range of conditions.

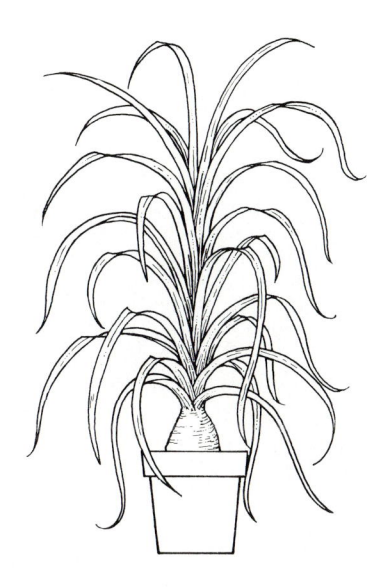

Beaucarnea

Beaucarnea recurvata
BOTTLE PONYTAIL
ELEPHANT FOOT
PONYTAIL PLANT

A peculiar plant that people either love or hate. Leaves are narrow, green and recurving. Small plants produce neat, firm bulbs at the base of their stems, the bulbs changing into more grotesque shapes as the plant ages. Because of its odd spreading habit of growth it is used more as an individual plant than as one of a group of plants.

New plants can be raised from seed sown in peat in warm conditions at almost any time of the year. Pot the resultant seedlings into small pots of peat initially, and into loam-based compost when they are of sufficient size. As an alternative to seed, new plants can be grown from the small bulbils that develop around the base of the parent.

The plant puts up with much ill-treatment provided the soil in its pot is not allowed to remain permanently saturated. Once established, plants respond to regular feeding while in active growth; none in winter.

Take care
Avoid cold and wetness in winter.

- Light shade
- Temp: 10-21°C (50-70°F)
- Water well in summer

MODERATE

Ceropegia woodii
HEARTS ENTANGLED
HEARTS ON A STRING
ROSARY VINE
STRING OF HEARTS

With the current fashion for hanging plants of all kinds this is the ideal plant to try, as it is so different from almost all other potted plants. Small, fleshy heart-shaped leaves are attached to wiry stems that hang perpendicularly from the plant. *C. woodii* is a hanging plant with no desire whatsoever to climb or do anything different. The leaves are mottled and grey-green in colour and the flowers are pink and tubular.

The common name of 'hearts entangled' comes from the manner in which the foliage twines around itself when the plants are growing actively. There is also the additional fascination of the gnarled bulbous growths that appear at soil level and along the stems of the plant, from which new growth sprouts. Indeed, the bulbils with growth attached can be used to propagate fresh plants, or they can be raised from cuttings.

When planting hanging containers it is advisable to propagate a batch of plants and to put five or so into each.

Take care
Avoid overwet winter conditions.

- Suspend in good light
- Temp: 13-18°C (55-65°F)
- Moist, but dry in winter

Ceropegia

Above: Ceropegia woodii is a natural trailing plant with a profusion of grey-coloured, heart-shaped leaves that have a succulent, puffed up appearance.

MODERATE

Chamaedorea elegans
(Neanthe bella)
GOOD-LUCK PALM
PARLOUR PALM

For people with limited space who wish to acquire a palm this is the answer, as the parlour palm presents a neat and compact plant throughout its life.

This plant is often used in bottle gardens, where it takes place of honour as the taller plant to give the miniature garden some height. One might add a word here to say that when planting bottle gardens it is most essential to ensure that small, non-invasive plants are selected.

The parlour palm should not be allowed to dry out excessively, although it should be a little on the dry side during the winter months, when growth is less active. It is important to ensure that the pot is well drained, and this will mean putting a layer of broken pieces of clay pot in the bottom of the new container before adding soil. Water poured onto the surface of the soil should be seen to flow fairly rapidly down through the mixture.

Take care
Avoid using chemicals on leaves.

- Light shade
- Temp: 16-21°C (60-70°F)
- Keep moist but well drained

Right: Cissus discolor is the aristocrat of the decorative pot-grown vines. It has a natural climbing habit and does best in warm, shaded and moist conditions.

Cissus

Cissus discolor
BEGONIA VINE
CLIMBING BEGONIA
TRAILING BEGONIA

This most beautiful climbing foliage plant has maroon undersides, and an upper leaf surface with a mixture of silver, red, green and other colours. Plants climb by means of clinging tendrils if given some support; to prevent gaps appearing as plants extend, pin some of the straying shoots down the stem.

A dry atmosphere can result in shrivelling of the leaves, as will exposure to bright sun; and very dry soil conditions also cause leaf problems. It seems necessary to renew older plants periodically rather than allow them to become straggly. Cuttings prepared from mature, firm leaves with stem attached will root in a temperature of 21°C (70°F) if put into small pots filled with moist peat. A closed propagating case and treating cuttings with rooting powder will also speed the process. Once rooted, cuttings should be potted into slightly larger pots using peaty mixture, and the soil thereafter kept moist but not waterlogged.

Take care
Avoid bright sun.

- Light shade
- Temp: 18-24°C (65-75°F)
- Keep moist and fed

MODERATE

Columnea banksii variegata
VARIEGATED GOLDFISH PLANT

The columneas are generally free-flowering plants, but the variegated form of *C. banksii* can be included among foliage plants, as it rarely produces flowers. The foliage is highly variegated, slow growing, and pendulous. The leaves are plump and fleshy, and attached to slender drooping stems; plants are seen at their best when suspended in a basket or hanging pot.

Cuttings are more difficult to root than the green forms of columnea. Short sections of stem with the lower leaves removed are best for propagating; treat with rooting powder before the cuttings, five to seven in small pots are inserted in a peat and sand mixture. A temperature of at least 21°C (70°F) is necessary and a propagator will be a great advantage. Due to the very slow rate of growth, it is necessary to allow the soil to dry reasonably between waterings. Feed with weak fertilizer, but never overdo it.

Take care
Keep reasonably warm.

- Light shade
- Temp: 16-21°C (60-70°F)
- Keep moist in summer

38

Cordyline

Left: A fine trailing plant with small, plump, green-and-white leaves, Columnea banksii variegata is best displayed in a hanging pot.

Below: This brilliantly coloured plant, Cordyline terminalis 'Firebrand', grows to 60-90cm (2-3ft) and needs light and warm conditions. Bad drainage may cause wet soil to discolour leaves.

Cordyline terminalis 'Firebrand'
FLAMING DRAGON TREE

Few foliage plants can match the rich red colouring of this cordyline though it is not the easiest of potted plants to care for. The colourful leaves are erect and spear-shaped.

Plants are grown by the nurseryman in a very open mixture composed mainly of pine leaf mould; this ensures that when water is poured onto the soil it drains freely through. It is preferable to use rain water, and to ensure that the soil is saturated each time. Avoid bone-dry conditions, but endeavour to allow some drying out of the soil between each soaking.

Good light is needed for *C. terminalis* to retain its bright colouring, but full sun through glass window-panes may cause scorching of foliage, so plants should be protected from such exposure. While new leaves are growing it will be important to feed plants at regular intervals, but it is not normally necessary to feed during the winter months.

Take care
Avoid excessive watering.

- Good light
- Temp: 18-24°C (65-75°F)
- Keep moist and fed

MODERATE

Cryptanthus bromelioides 'It'
EARTH STAR
RAINBOW-STAR

A comparatively recent introduction that resembles *C. tricolor*, but is of much bolder pink and is more attractive, although individual plants vary in brightness of colour. The new variety also grows closer to the pot. The leaves are stiffer in appearance, begin with a thick base attached to a short main stem, and taper to a point.

Cryptanthuses, like all bromeliads, require to be potted into a very open, free-draining mixture. One suggestion is to prepare a mixture of coarse leaf mould and a peaty houseplant potting mixture and to pot the plants in this, using small containers. Treated tree bark that is not too coarse may be used as a substitute for leaf mould. Place a few pieces of broken pot in the bottom of the container before introducing the soil. When watering these plants it is important that they have a thorough soak and then be allowed to dry reasonably before more is given. Clean rain water will be ideal.

Take care
Avoid sodden root conditions.

- Light shade
- Temp: 16-21° C (60-70°F)
- Keep on dry side

Right: Cryptanthus bromelioides 'It' is neat and compact; ideal for small plant gardens in bottles. It is admired for its bold and vibrant pink colour.

Cryptanthus

Cryptanthus bromelioides tricolor
EARTH STAR
RAINBOW-STAR

The pink, green and white colouring of this plant can be spectacular in well-grown specimens, but they are not easy plants to care for. Although grouped with the other flatter growing cryptanthuses under the same common name of earth star, these have a slightly different habit of growth. The centre of the plant tends to extend upwards, and new plant growth sprouts from the side of the parent rosette. If these side growths are left attached to the parent a full and handsome plant will in time develop; or they can be removed when of reasonable size by pulling them sideways; it is then simple to press the pieces into peaty mixture for them to produce roots.

Almost all cryptanthuses are terrestrial and are seen at their best when nestled in the crevices of an old tree stump, or surrounded by a few stones. *C. tricolor*, with its more open habit of growing, can also be effective in a hanging pot or basket.

Take care
Avoid wet and cold conditions.

- Light shade
- Temp: 16-21°C (60-70°F)
- Keep on dry side

Top: The star-shaped, radiating growth of Cryptanthus bromelioides tricolor gives it the common name of 'earth star'. This plant is striped with green, white and pink.

MODERATE

Right: A fine bromeliad from South America, Cryptanthus 'Foster's Favourite' has stiff, unbending leaves forming a star shape.

Cryptanthus 'Foster's Favourite'
EARTH STAR

Here is another splendid example from the fine bromeliad family from tropical South America. Named after a famous American nurseryman, this variety tends to be much larger than most cryptanthus plants and produces long leaves with a pheasant-feather pattern. The thick, fleshy leaves have the shape of a dagger blade and radiate from a short central stem.

In their natural habitat these plants grow on the floor of the forest among old tree stumps and boulders, so they are capable of withstanding rough treatment. But remember the old maxim – which applies to almost all indoor plants – that when low temperatures prevail or plants are likely to be exposed to trying conditions they will fare much better if kept on the dry side. In fact, no bromeliads will prosper if roots are confined to pots that are permanently saturated. An open potting mixture is essential so that water can drain through very freely.

Take care
Never overwater.

- Light shade
- Temp: 16-21°C (60-70°F)
- Avoid excessive watering

Dieffenbachia amoena
DUMB CANE
MOTHER-IN-LAW'S TONGUE PLANT
TUFTROOT

This is possibly the largest of the dieffenbachias. The striking grey-green leaves with central colouring of speckled white and green will add much to any collection of indoor plants, but be warned – mature plants can attain a height of 1.2-1.5m (4-5ft) with a wide spread. However, stout stems can be cut out with a small saw. When carrying out any sort of work on dieffenbachias, though, gloves should be worn to prevent any sap getting onto one's skin. Even moving plants that have

42

Dieffenbachia

wet foliage may result in skin disorders. Also keep plants out of reach of children and pets. The common name of dumb cane derives from the fact that if the sap of the plant gets into one's mouth it will cause loss of speech. Fortunately, such an occurrence is unlikely, as the sap has a very nasty odour.

A variety of *D. amoena*, 'Tropic Snow', differs from the normal type in that its leaves are stiffer in appearance and have a greater area of white. The leaves are also inclined to be brittle and are easily damaged if carelessly handled. When cleaning the plant, therefore, place a supporting hand beneath the leaves as you wipe the surface with a soft cloth.

Take care
Never get sap onto your skin.

- ☐ Light shade
- ☐ Temp: 18-24°C (65-75°F)
- ☐ Keep moist and fed

Below: Dieffenbachia amoena 'Tropic Snow' is a bold foliage plant with stout green-and-white leaves. This plant needs warm, moist and shady conditions.

MODERATE

Dieffenbachia maculata
DUMB CANE
MOTHER-IN-LAW'S TONGUE PLANT
TUFTROOT

This is one of the traditional warm greenhouse plants that may have been found in many a Victorian conservatory at the turn of the century when exotic plants were all the rage. Not seen so frequently today, *D. maculata* has speckled yellowish-green colouring and grows to a height of 90cm (3ft) when given proper care. If the top of the plant is removed when young, the plant will produce numerous side growths that will make it a more attractive shape. An effective display plant when carefully grown.

In common with all the many fine dieffenbachias these plants require warm and humid conditions. Permanently saturated soil must be avoided, but it is important that the pot is well watered with each application, and surplus water is seen to drain through the bottom of the pot. It is equally important that the soil should dry reasonably before further water is given.

Take care
Avoid low temperatures.

- Light shade
- Temp: 18-24°C (65-75°F)
- Keep moist and fed

Dieffenbachia

Left: The forerunner of the more compact 'dumb canes', Dieffenbachia maculata 'Exotica' produces young growth at the base of the stem.

Above: Dieffenbachia maculata is a well-established plant of graceful appearance with pale green speckled foliage.

Dieffenbachia maculata 'Exotica'
DUMB CANE
MOTHER-IN-LAW'S TONGUE PLANT
TUFTROOT

The introduction of this superb houseplant was something of a revolution as far as dieffenbachias were concerned. Previous plants of this kind were decidedly difficult subjects to grow at the nurseries, to transport and to keep once they arrived at the home of the purchaser; they were also inclined to be too large for the average room of today.

This is a neat plant growing to a maximum of 60cm (2ft) – much more suitable for indoors – and with a much tougher constitution. It tolerates lower temperatures, and if not too wet does not seem to suffer. It produces clusters of young plants at the base of the parent stem, and can be propagated easily by removing the basal shoots and planting them separately in small pots filled with peat. Once rooted they should be potted in a peaty houseplant compost. Shoots can often be removed with roots attached, but gloves should be worn.

Take care
Never get sap onto your skin.

- ☐ Light shade
- ☐ Temp: 16-21°C (60-70°F)
- ☐ Keep moist and fed

45

MODERATE

Dizygotheca elegantissima
(Aralia elegantissima)
FALSE ARALIA

Also known as *Aralia elegantissima*, this is one of the most attractive of the purely foliage plants, having dark green, almost black, colouring to its leaves. Graceful leaves radiate from stiff, upright stems that will attain a height of about 3m (10ft). As the plant ages it loses its delicate foliage and produces leaves that are much larger and coarser in appearance. One can remove the upper section of stem, and new growth will revert to the original delicate appearance.

Warm conditions with no drop in temperature are important; water thoroughly, soaking the soil, and allow it to dry reasonably before repeating. Feed in spring and summer, less in winter.

Mealy bug can be treated with a liquid insecticide; affected areas should be thoroughly saturated with the spray. Root mealy bugs can be seen as a whitish powder around the roots; to clear these, liquid insecticide should be watered in.

Take care
Avoid fluctuating temperatures.

- ☐ Light shade
- ☐ Temp: 18-21°C (65-70°F)
- ☐ Keep moist

Above: Dizygotheca elegantissima is a striking plant with very dark green, almost black, foliage that is delicate on young plants but becomes coarse with age.

Dracaena deremensis
STRIPED DRACAENA

There are numerous improved forms of this dracaena, all erect with broad, pointed leaves up to 60cm (2ft) long. The variations are mostly in leaf colour: *D. deremensis* 'Bausei' has a dark green margin and glistening white centre; in *D. deremensis* 'Souvenir de Schriever' the top-most rosette of leaves is bright yellow, but the leaves revert to the grey-green with white stripes of the parent plant as they age.

An unfortunate aspect of this type of dracaena is that they shed lower leaves as they increase in height, so that they take on a palm-like

Dracaena

Above: There are several varieties of the elegant and eye-catching Dracaena deremensis. The plant creates an ideal 'architectural' focal point in a large room.

appearance with tufts of leaves at the top of otherwise bare stems. Although loss of lower leaves is a natural process, the incidence of drying and falling leaves will be aggravated by excessive watering. Water thoroughly, and then allow the soil to dry reasonably before repeating. These are hungry plants and will be in need of regular feeding, with loam-based soil recommended for potting on.

Take care
Never allow to become too wet.

- Light
- Temp: 16-21°C (60-70°F)
- Keep on the dry side

Dracaena deremensis 'Warneckii'

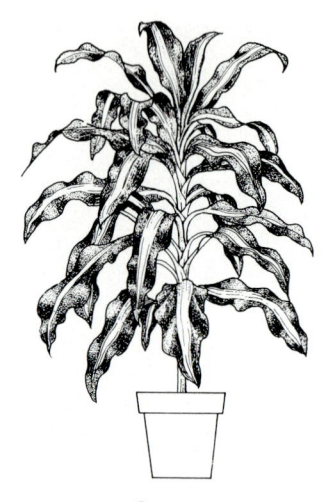

MODERATE

Dracaena fragrans
CORN PALM

The green-foliaged type is seldom offered for sale, but there are two important cultivars. The easiest to care for is *D. fragrans* 'Massangeana', which has broad mustard-coloured leaves attached to stout central stems; and presenting a little more difficulty there is *D. fragrans* 'Victoria' with brighter creamy-gold colouring.

As with most dracaenas there will be loss of lower leaves as plants increase in height, but plants eventually take on a stately, palm-like appearance.

Fortunately, few pests trouble these plants, but there is the occasional possibility of mealy bugs finding their way into the less accessible parts that lie between the base of the leaf and the stem of the plant. Prepare malathion solution and with the aid of a hand sprayer inject the insecticide down among the base of the leaves. As with all activities involving insecticides, wear rubber gloves and take all recommended precautions.

Take care
Feed established plants well.

- Light shade
- Temp: 18-24°C (65-75°F)
- Keep moist and fed

Right: Dracaena marginata tricolor has narrow leaves of striking colours. Good light helps colour develop. Soil should be kept on the dry side to prevent leaf drop.

Dracaena

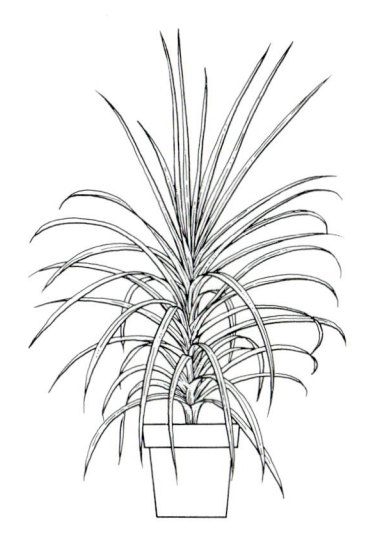

Dracaena marginata tricolor
VARIEGATED MADAGASCAR DRAGON TREE
VARIEGATED SILHOUETTE PLANT

This plant has a natural tendency to shed lower leaves as it increases in height. Nevertheless, it can be an elegant plant if carefully grown, having attractive light and darker colouring running along the entire length of the slender, pointed leaves.

The main stem of the plant will need a supporting cane to remain upright. Plants sometimes produce young shoots naturally along the main stem so that multiheaded plants result. Alternatively, one can remove the growing tip of the main stem when the plant is about 60cm (2ft) tall, so that branching is encouraged. If plants are grown in soil that is constantly saturated, the incidence of leaf damage will be much increased. The soil for these plants should always be on the dry side, especially so during winter.

Feeding is not desperately important, but weak liquid fertilizer during the spring and summer months will do no harm; winter feeding is not advised.

Take care
Keep warm, light and dry.

- Good light
- Temp: 16-21°C (60-70°F)
- Avoid wet conditions

MODERATE

Ficus benjamina
BENJAMIN TREE
JAVA FIG
SMALL-LEAVED RUBBER TREE
WEEPING FIG

Of very graceful weeping habit, *F. benjamina* will develop into tree size if provided with the right conditions. However, excess growth can be trimmed out at any time. To maintain plants in good condition with their glossy leaves gleaming it is important to feed them well while in active growth, and to pot them on into loam-based mixture as required. Little feeding and no potting should be done in winter, and it is also wise during this period to water more sparingly unless the plants are drying out in hot rooms. The weeping fig has a tendency to shed leaves in poorly lit situations.

Not many pests affect ficus plants, but scale insects seem to favour *F. benjamina*. These are either dark or light brown in colour and cling to stems and the undersides of leaves. Another sign of their presence will be dark sooty deposits on leaves below where the pests are clinging. It is best to wash them off with malathion.

Take care
Avoid placing in dark areas.

- Good light, no direct sun
- Temp: 16-21°C (60-70°F)
- Keep moist and fed

Above: The elegant 'weeping fig', Ficus benjamina, has glossy green foliage and naturally cascading branches – a combination that produces one of the finest foliage plants.

Below: Ficus benjamina 'Hawaii' is similar in appearance to the 'weeping fig' but has a more erect habit. The bright leaves are seen at their best in good light.

Ficus

Ficus benjamina 'Hawaii'
VARIEGATED WEEPING FIG

A recent introduction with white- and-green variegated leaves that seems likely to become a very successful indoor subject.

To get the best from these plants they need good light without bright sun, and the temperature should not fall below 16°C (60°F). Watering should follow the standard procedure for larger indoor plants, ie well watered from the top with surplus water clearly seen to drain out of the bottom of the container. The plant should then be left until the soil has dried out to a reasonable degree before watering again.

Younger plants should be provided with a supporting stake and the plant tied to the stake as new growth develops. However, a few strands should be allowed to hang over so that a plant with weeping growth all the way up results.

Like the green *F. benjamina*, this will tend to shed leaves at a rather alarming rate if it is placed in too dark a location.

Take care
Avoid placing in dark areas.

- Light shade
- Temp: 16-21°C (60-70°F)
- Keep moist and fed

MODERATE

Above: Ficus elastica 'Europa' is the best variegated form of broad-leaved rubber plant. It has remarkably fine colouring and is relatively easy to care for.

Below: Leaf shape gives the common name of 'fiddle leaf fig' to Ficus lyrata, one of the boldest and most vigorous indoor plants. The leaves are glossy green.

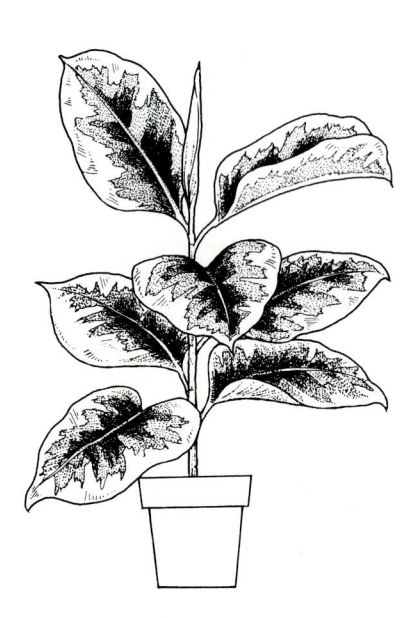

Ficus elastica 'Europa'
VARIEGATED RUBBER PLANT

Far and away the best variegated broad-leaved rubber plant ever to be produced. Leaf colouring is a bright cream and green and the

Ficus

stems are bold and upright. Unlike previous variegated rubber plants this one does not have the usual tendency to develop brown discolouration along its leaf margins, and it is altogether more vigorous.

Taller plants will require supporting stakes, and ample watering and feeding while new leaves are being produced. This should be all year except during the winter months. However, some plants are slow to get on the move and such plants should be watered with care until it is seen that new leaves are on the way at the top of the stem.

All the broad-leaved rubber plants will be the better for cleaning with a damp cloth or sponge periodically, but one should not be too enthusiastic when it comes to use of chemical cleaners.

Take care
Avoid wet winter conditions.

- □ Good light
- □ Temp: 16-21°C (60-70°F)
- □ Keep moist and fed

Ficus lyrata
FIDDLE LEAF FIG

One of the more majestic members of the big family, *F. lyrata* develops into a small branching tree. Leaves are glossy green with prominent veins and, as the common name suggests, are shaped like the body of a violin. The original single stem of the plant will naturally shed lower leaves and the plant will produce leaf buds in the axils of the topmost four to six leaves, and in time these will become the branches of the tree.

It is important to seek out plants that have fresh, dark green leaves rather than those that may be marked or discoloured. Indoors they should be offered reasonable light and warmth, and in their early stages of development they will need careful watering; the plants are best kept on the dry side rather than too wet. More mature plants in larger pots will require more watering and more frequent feeding, with less of both being given in winter. The plant can be pruned at any time to improve its shape.

Take care
Avoid cold draughts.

- □ Light shade
- □ Temp: 16-21°C (60-70°F)
- □ Keep moist and fed

53

MODERATE

Gynura sarmentosa
VELVET PLANT

Scented flowers are a bonus with almost all plants, but the gynuras have been blessed with a scent that is obnoxious enough to be almost damaging to the senses. Weedy flowers appear in summer and should be removed before they have a chance to open. However, there are almost always compensations in nature and the gynuras are favoured with violet-tinged foliage that is hairy and very striking when seen in sunlight. They will grow at a rampant pace in light conditions if they are being watered carefully and fed regularly. Given a supporting cane plants can be encouraged to climb, but they are seen at their best when trailing from a pot or basket.

Untidy growth can be trimmed back at almost any time, and firm pieces may be used for propagating new plants. This should be done regularly as older plants tend to become untidy and lose their bright colouring. It is best to put several cuttings in each pot and to pinch out tips for bushy plants.

Take care
Replace older plants every year.

- Good light
- Temp: 13-18°C (55-65°F)
- Keep moist and fed

Above: The fragile and elegant Howeia forsteriana provides an ideal, decorative plant for the home. Proceed with caution if using any chemical treatments.

Below: Gynura sarmentosa is a member of the nettle family. The leaves are tinged with purple, with a generous covering of tiny hairs that give the plant a rich glow of colour when seen in sunlight.

Howeia

Howeia forsteriana
(Kentia forsteriana)
KENTIA PALM
PARADISE PALM
THATCH-LEAF PALM

Howeia forsteriana is one of the most elegant and interesting of all the plants grown in pots for indoor decoration, but it is tending to become increasingly expensive. Most of the seed for growing these plants commercially still comes from their natural home of Lord Howe Island in the South Pacific.

To grow well, all palms need an open, fibrous potting mixture, and it is also a good idea to put a layer of clay pot shards in the base of the container.

The long upright leaves of these plants are sensitive to many of the chemicals used for controlling pests and for cleaning foliage, so it is wise to test any products on a small section of the plant before going in at the deep end and treating it all over. When testing such chemicals one should wait for at least a week to see what the reaction may be. It is also very unwise to expose plants to full sun or to cold conditions following any application of chemicals.

Take care
Avoid wet winter conditions.

- Light shade
- Temp: 16-21°C (60-70°F)
- Water and feed well in summer

MODERATE

Hypoestes sanguinolenta
FLAMINGO PLANT
FRECKLE FACE
MEASLES PLANT
PINK-DOT PLANT
POLKA DOT PLANT

In the last few years the hypoestes has enjoyed a new lease of life through the introduction of a much more colourful cultivar with a greater proportion of pink in its leaves.

Plants are easy to manage, although they frequently suffer through being confined to pots too small for the amount of growth that these quick growers will normally produce. Any purchased plant that appears to be in too small a pot should be potted into a larger one without delay. Use loam-based potting soil, as peat mixtures can be fatal for this plant if they dry out excessively. Also, it is wise to remove the growing tips so that plants branch and become more attractive. Untidy or overgrown stems can be removed at any time, and firm pieces about 10cm (4in) long can be used for propagation.

Extremely dry soil will cause loss of lower leaves, so check daily to ensure that the soil is moist. (See page 94 for illustration.)

Take care
Avoid drying out of soil.

- Good light
- Temp: 10-16°C (50-60°F)
- Keep moist and fed

Maranta

Maranta leuconeura erythrophylla
HERRINGBONE PLANT
PRAYER PLANT

With reddish-brown colouring and intricately patterned, rounded leaves, this is one of the more attractive smaller plants. Exotic colouring immediately suggests that it is difficult, but the reverse is true if sufficient warmth is maintained and reasonable care given.

These plants are best grown naturally with foliage trailing where it will. Unless the leaves are misted twice daily, hanging containers will usually prove to be too dry a location for them; it will be better to grow plants at a lower level. To improve humidity around the plant place the pot in a larger container with moist peat packed between the two pots.

Peaty mixture is essential when potting on, but one should not be too hasty in transferring plants to very large pots. Fertilizer should be very weak and given with each watering rather than in a few heavy doses.

In time the plants will become ragged and it may then be wise to start again with new cuttings.

Take care
Avoid bright sunlight.

- Light shade
- Temp: 18-24°C (65-75°F)
- Moist soil and atmosphere

Left: Intricately marked, reddish-brown and green-coloured leaves make Maranta leuconeura erythrophylla a very colourful and vivid foliage plant.

MODERATE

Above: With pale green, darkly spotted leaves, Maranta leuconeura kerchoviana is among the easiest of the marantas to care for. For best results, offer moisture, shade and warmth.

Maranta leuconeura kerchoviana
PRAYER PLANT
RABBIT'S-FOOT
RABBIT'S TRACKS

Dark spots on grey-green leaves give this plant its unusual common name; the dark spots are said to resemble the tracks left by a rabbit. One of the older established houseplants, it is one of the easiest of this family to care for. It needs protection from direct sunlight and must be reasonably warm. Frequent feeding with weak liquid fertilizer is best, and one should use a peaty

potting mixture.
   When watering, the soil should be moist but not totally saturated for very long periods, especially in winter. The danger with peat mixtures is that they will soak up very much more water than the plant is ever likely to need and will become totally waterlogged – a dangerous condition for most plants. For this reason plants should not be watered from the bottom and allowed to absorb water from the pot saucer. It is very much better to water into the top of the pot, giving sufficient to ensure that surplus drains away.

Take care
Avoid bright sunlight.

- Shade
- Temp: 16-21°C (60-70°F)
- Moist soil and atmosphere

Below: Monstera deliciosa has interesting leaves which are perforated in older plants and deeply cut along the margins. Strong aerial roots are produced.

Monstera deliciosa
CUT-LEAF PHILODENDRON
FRUIT SALAD PLANT
MEXICAN BREADFRUIT
SPLIT-LEAF PHILODENDRON
SWISS CHEESE PLANT
WINDOW PLANT

The naturally glossy green leaves with attractive deep serrations make the monsteras among the most popular of all indoor foliage plants. The aerial roots produced from the stems of more mature plants are an interesting and often perplexing feature. Removing some excess roots will not be harmful, but in most instances it is better to tie the roots neatly to the stem of the plant and to guide them into the pot soil.
   As plants mature they will naturally produce serrated leaves, but darker growing conditions can result in leaves that are smaller and complete, rather than cut out. Bright sunlight magnified by window glass can cause scorching of foliage and should be avoided, particularly while soft new leaves are maturing.
   Monsteras belong to the Araceae family and in their natural jungle environment will tend to scramble along the floor before finding a tree trunk to climb.

Take care
Avoid exposure to direct sunlight.

- Light shade
- Temp: 16-21°C (60-70°F)
- Moist roots, regular feeding

MODERATE

Neoregelia carolinae tricolor
BLUSHING BROMELIAD
CARTWHEEL PLANT

Although it does produce small and inconspicuous flowers in the centre of the rosette of leaves (the 'urn' or 'vase') this is very much a foliage plant. Overlapping leaves radiate from a short central trunk and are spectacularly striped in cream and green with the added attraction, as the flowers begin to appear, of the shorter central leaves and the base of larger leaves turning a brilliant shade of red.

Following this colourful display the main rosette will naturally deteriorate and in time will have to be cut away from the small trunk to which it is attached. Take care that the small plant or plants forming around the base of the trunk are not damaged during this operation, as these will be the plants of the future. Leave the young plantlets attached to the stump to grow on or, in preference, remove them when they have developed several leaves of their own and pot them into peaty mixture.

Take care
Periodically change the water in the central urn of leaves.

- Good light
- Temp: 13-18°C (55-65°F)
- Dry at roots, urn filled

Right: A member of the bromeliad family, Neoregelia carolinae tricolor *is a spectacular plant with flat rosettes of leaves which overlap at their base to make a watertight urn for water.*

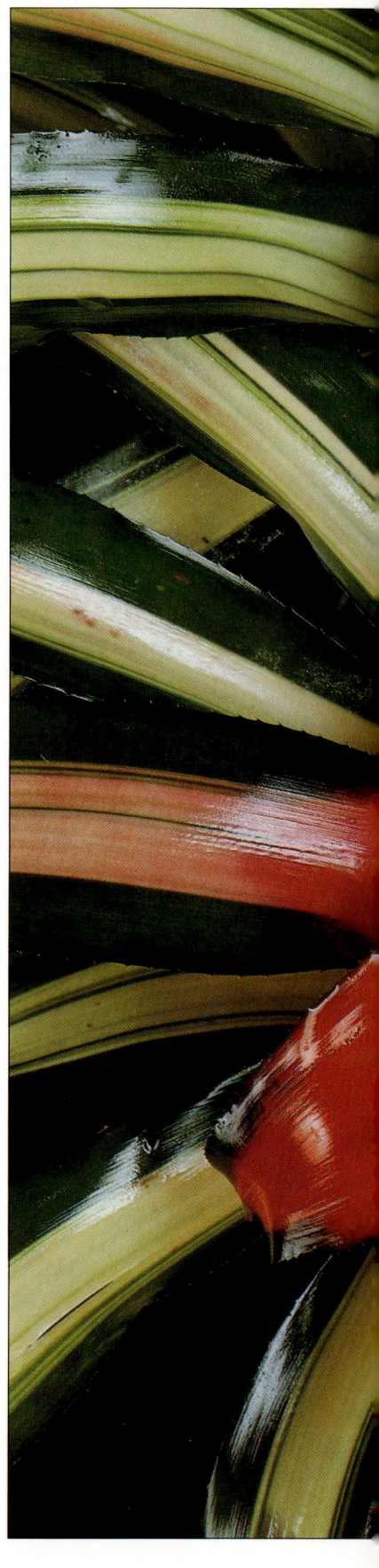

60

Neoregelia

MODERATE

Pandanus baptiste
SCREW PINE

This is probably the best-protected plant of them all. Vicious barbs are along the margins of the leaves, and a barbed keel runs the length of the underside of each leaf; all are capable of drawing blood if carelessly handled. However, the screw pine has incredible bright yellow markings, which sets it apart from almost every other plant. The large recurving leaves are produced from a very stout trunk and will attain a length of 1.8m (6ft) and a width of 15cm (6in) or more when roots are confined to a pot. Should you be considering one of these for your home, be sure that you have a place large enough to accommodate it.

Older plants take on a further interesting dimension when they produce stout anchor roots from the main trunk; these extend in the manner of tent guy ropes around the plant to anchor it when hurricane winds hit its natural tropical island home. Surprisingly, these plants can flourish when underfed and underwatered.

Take care
Approach with caution.

- Good light
- Temp: 16-21°C (60-70°F)
- Avoid too wet conditions

Right: Plants such as Pandanus baptiste, pictured here, need ample space. The leaves have spined margins and a spined keel on their underside.

Above: Peperomia griseoargentea has glossy grey-coloured leaves which are produced in quantity but remain small in size to form neat and compact plants.

Peperomia

Peperomia griseoargentea
(Peperomia hederifolia)
IVY-LEAF PEPEROMIA
PLATINUM PEPEROMIA
RADIATOR PLANT
SILVER RIPPLE
SILVER-LEAF PEPEROMIA

Unusual glossy grey colouring sets *P. griseoargentea* apart from most other indoor plants. Stalked leaves are rounded in shape and emerge from soil level, there being no stem to speak of. At one time a great favourite in the houseplant league it now seems to have waned a little, probably resulting from other more interesting plants coming along to take its place. One of its main benefits lies in the fact that it occupies little space and is ideal for including in small planted arrangements. For example, they are ideal for carboys, which can only be planted with small plants that are not too invasive. Vigorous plants will quickly invade the growing space of every plant in the container.

This peperomia will enjoy a watering routine that allows the soil to dry out, but not bone dry, between each watering. It will also respond well to frequent weak feeds, but needs no feeding and less water in winter.

Take care
Avoid wet and cold combination.

☐ Light shade
☐ Temp: 16-21°C (60-70°F)
☐ Keep moist and fed

MODERATE

Philodendron bipinnatifidum
FIDDLELEAF PHILODENDRON
HORSEHEAD PHILODENDRON
PANDA PLANT
TREE PHILODENDRON

There are numerous philodendrons of similar type to this one, all requiring ample space for their radiating leaves once they reach maturity. Because of their habit of growth these are essentially individual plants to be placed on their own rather than as part of a collection. Leaves are glossy green in colour and deeply cut along their margins, and held on stout petioles attached to very solid, short trunks. In time aerial roots will be produced from the trunk; direct these into the pot soil when they are long enough. With older plants it may be necessary to remove some of these aerial roots, or they can be allowed to trail into a dish of water placed alongside.

Ample watering is a must, with marginally less being given in winter; and feeding should not be neglected. When potting on use a mixture containing some loam, as these are quite greedy plants. Most of them are raised from seed and young plants are usually available.

Take care
These plants need space.

- Shade
- Temp: 16-21°C (60-70°F)
- Keep wet and fed

Above: When young, Philodendron bipinnatifidum has a tendency to be weedy; however, the plant becomes majestic with age. For best results, keep the soil moist.

Phoenix

Phoenix canariensis
CANARY DATE PALM
CANARY ISLAND DATE
FEATHER PALM

Below: Phoenix canariensis is a tough, tropical palm with coarse foliage. It has a solid, gnarled trunk that becomes a principal feature as the plant ages.

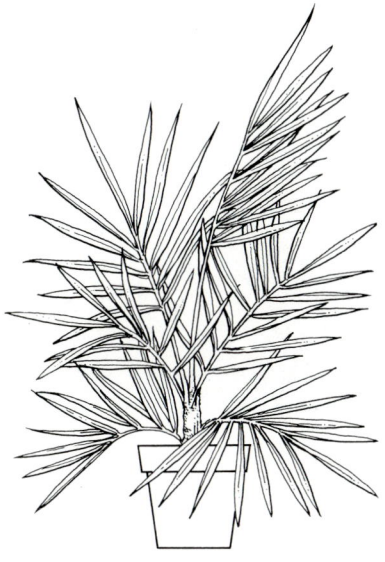

In their tropical habitat these stately palms will grow to 9-12m (30-40ft) in height, but they are less vigorous when their roots are confined to pots. Leaves are coarse and open, and attached to short, stout trunks. Leaves have short petioles armed with vicious short spines, which make it necessary to handle the plant with care. Older plants are normally beyond the purse of the average person, so seek out plants of more modest size when shopping.

Smaller plants can be potted on into loam-based potting soil. Good drainage is essential, so broken flower pots or some other form of drainage material ought to be placed in the bottom of the pot before any soil is introduced. Well-drained soil is needed, but regular and thorough watering will be of the utmost importance while plants are actively growing. During growth, feed plants at regular intervals using a proprietary fertilizer and following the maker's directions.

Take care
Check occasionally for red spider.

- Good light
- Temp: 16-21°C (60-70°F)
- Keep moist

MODERATE

Above: When mature, the Phoenix roebelinii palm is among the most impressive of all foliage plants, with fine leaves radiating from a central stem.

Select loam-based potting mixture with some body to it. Good drainage will ensure that the soil in the pot will remain fresh and well aerated, which is essential if palm roots are not to rot and die. During the summer, plants can go out of doors in a sheltered, sunny location.

Not many pests bother this plant, but the ubiquitous red spider will usually be lurking around if the growing conditions tend to be very hot and dry. One should suspect their presence if plants become harder in appearance and develop paler colouring than usual. Some insecticides are harmful to palm plants, therefore it is wise to check suitability with your supplier before purchasing.

Phoenix roebelinii
FEATHER PALM
MINIATURE DATE PALM
PYGMY DATE PALM
ROEBELIN PALM

Take care
Ensure soil is well drained.

- Good light
- Temp: 16-21°C (60-70°F)
- Keep moist

This species is not unlike *P. canariensis* as a young plant, but later is more feathery and delicate and less coarse in appearance. It is also less robust, retains its shape better, and will attain a height of around 1.5m (5ft) when grown.

Polyscias

Polyscias balfouriana
BALFOUR ARALIA
DINNER PLATE ARALIA

This is another painfully slow grower that will take at least 10 years to reach 3m (10ft) in height, but in limited space this could be an advantage. Stems are woody and the leaf colouring is variegated white and green. Growth is very erect and plants seldom need to be staked. As the plant ages and increases in height, the lower stem will have a natural tendency to shed leaves.

Red spider mites seem to find this plant particularly appetizing. Although minute in size, these pests can increase at an alarming rate and completely blanket the plant to such an extent that it may well not recover. The layman often finds it difficult to believe that such minute pests can be so destructive. When they are detected, take action right away, by preparing a recommended insecticide solution and thoroughly saturating the undersides of all foliage. This task ought to be done out of doors on a warm day, and rubber gloves and a mask worn.

Take care
Check for pests under leaves.

- Light shade
- Temp: 16-21°C (60-70°F)
- Keep moist and fed

Below: The leaves of Polyscias balfouriana 'Pinnochio' are round with creamy-yellow and green variegations. Stems are woody and the plant is generally slow growing.

MODERATE

Sansevieria trifasciata 'Golden Hahnii'
GOLDEN BIRD'S NEST

Because this plant is incredibly slow-growing, it may be difficult to find on sale. There is also a plain green *S. trifasciata* 'Hahnii', but it is not in the least attractive compared to the golden-coloured variety. Both make neat rosettes of overlapping leaves 10cm (4in) in length.

One of the best homes for them is a dry bottle garden; or they can be used in a dish garden. Like the more conventional sansevierias, both 'Hahnii' varieties abhor wet conditions, and will quickly succumb should the prevailing conditions offer a combination of wet and cold. Warm and dry will suit them very much better; in winter they will go for weeks on end without any water, and in some situations they could well go through the winter completely dry, as do most of the cacti and succulents. Feeding is not important, but a loam-based potting mix will be much better than one that is entirely peat.

Take care
Avoid cold and wetness.

- Good light
- Temp: 16-21°C (60-70°F)
- Avoid overwatering

Right: A naturally trailing succulent plant, Sedum morganianum has bluish-grey leaves that hang perpendicularly from the suspended growing pot.

Sedum

Sedum morganianum
BURRO'S TAIL
DONKEY'S TAIL
HORSE'S TAIL
LAMB'S TAIL

The burro's tail is a rather fascinating plant in that the fleshy leaves are closely grouped on slender hanging stems that give the strands of plants the appearance of a very meticulously plaited length of rope. One problem is that the small pads of growth are easily dislodged with handling. It should be grown in a hanging pot or basket.

However, suspending small pots overhead is fraught with danger as far as the plants are concerned, as it is extremely difficult to water them satisfactorily, and one also tends to forget them. When utilizing burro's tail as a hanging plant it is suggested that several small plants be put into the same container to give a bolder display and make their care easier. Mention is made above of hanging plants *above* one's head, but it is better to hang them at about head level so that they can be easily checked and tended. Use porous potting mixture, and keep plants on the dry side and in good light.

Take care
Handle carefully in transit.

- Light shade
- Temp: 13-18°C (55-65°F)
- Keep on dry side

DIFFICULT

Difficult to Grow

The plants in this section are generally more difficult to grow than other species because they demand high and constant temperatures and humidity. These conditions are often difficult to achieve in centrally heated homes where the atmosphere tends to be dry and temperatures can fluctuate so much between day and night. Bear in mind that, even if you cannot achieve the ideal temperature, you must maintain a humid environment when growing those plants with thin and papery leaves.

The houseplants featured here include some of the most interesting and beautifully-leaved of all foliage plants, from the vibrantly coloured peacock plant (*Calathea makoyana*) to the fascinating Venus's flytrap (*Dionaea muscipula*).

Alocasia

Alocasia indica
ELEPHANT'S EAR

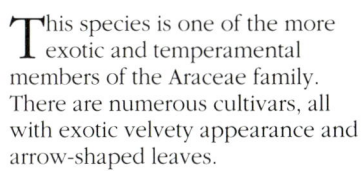

This species is one of the more exotic and temperamental members of the Araceae family. There are numerous cultivars, all with exotic velvety appearance and arrow-shaped leaves.

Their most important needs are for a temperature of around 24°C (75°F) and for a humid atmosphere. The soil in the pot must be kept moist at all times, and it is essential that the surrounding atmosphere is also moist; this will mean placing the plant on a large tray filled with gravel, which should be kept permanently wet. The tray can contain water, but the level should never be up to the surface of the pebbles so that the plant pot is actually standing in water. Plants allowed to stand in water become waterlogged, and will rot and die. Feeding is not important, but it will do no harm if liquid fertilizer is given periodically.

Take care
Keep plants out of draughts and away from hot radiators.

- Light shade
- Temp: 18-24°C (65-75°F)
- Keep moist

Left: Most appropriate for the skilled plant person, Alocasia indica needs high humidity and constant warmth.

DIFFICULT

Right: The large, boldly veined leaves of Anthurium crystallinum are impressive and best when supported. A subject suited for very warm, humid conditions.

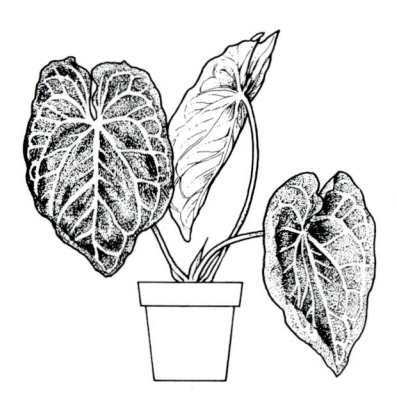

Anthurium crystallinum
CRYSTAL ANTHURIUM
STRAP FLOWER

This plant is among the more temperamental foliage plants. It does produce a flower, but this is in fact a thin rat's tail. However, the rat's tail has the important function of producing seed, from which new plants can be raised relatively easily in a high temperature. The patterned, heart-shaped leaves are very large and spectacular and usually have to be supported if they are to show to their best advantage.

High temperature, lightly shaded location and humid atmosphere are their principal needs. Roots should at no time dry out. Regular feeding will maintain foliage in brighter colour and better condition. Potting mixture containing a percentage of loam should be used and the pot should be provided with drainage material. Although plants must not dry at their roots, it is essential that water should drain away freely.

Pests are not a problem. Avoid handling, or cleaning the leaves with chemical concoctions.

Take care
Maintain high humidity.

- Light shade
- Temp: 18-24°C (65-75°F)
- Moist atmosphere

Right: The smooth, pale green leaves of Asplenium nidus radiate from the centre in an attractive arrangement.

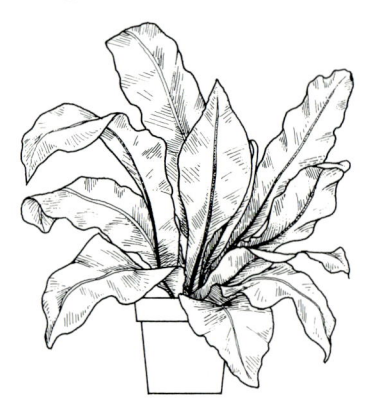

Asplenium nidus
BIRD'S NEST FERN
NEST FERN

As small plants these are not very exciting, but once they have been advanced to pot sizes of around 18cm (7in) they have few

Asplenium

equals. But the growing of these plants to perfection is one of the more difficult exercises in horticulture. Surrounding objects touching tender leaves will almost certainly cause irreparable damage, as will spraying foliage with unsuitable chemicals, or the presence of slugs.

Leaves can be kept in good order if a temperature of around 21°C (70°F) is maintained and plants enjoy good light but not direct sun. Open, peaty mixture is needed when potting, and water applied to the top of the soil should immediately flow through. Frequent feeding of established plants with weak fertilizer is preferred to infrequent heavier doses. Keep soil moist.

Scale insects can be seen as dark brown or flesh-coloured spots adhering to the area around the midrib of the leaf. These can be sponged off with malathion.

Take care
Never handle young foliage.

- Shade
- Temp: 18-24°C (65-75°F)
- Moist roots and surroundings

DIFFICULT

Calathea

Caladium hybrids
ANGELS' WINGS
ELEPHANT'S EARS

There is a wide variety of these hybrids, all in need of some cosseting if they are to succeed. Adequate temperature is essential, and they are sensitive to the effects of bright sun through clear glass.

When potting it is important to use a high proportion of peat that will drain freely. Repot over-wintered tubers soon after they have produced their first new growth. Old soil should be teased gently away, care being taken not to damage any new roots that may be forming. Rather than transfer plants to very large pots it is better, having removed much of the old soil, to repot the plant into the same container using fresh mixture.

Leaves of these plants will not tolerate any cleaning. When buying plants, get them from a reliable retailer with heated premises, as cold conditions for only a short time can be fatal. Although arum-type flowers are produced, there are unattractive and should be removed.

Take care
Provide adequate storage warmth.

- Light shade
- Temp: 18-24°C (65-75°F)
- Keep moist when in leaf

Left: The 'peacock plant', Calathea makoyana, has large, oval-shaped leaves that are intricately patterned and paper thin. Stout stalks spring from soil level.

Calathea makoyana
(Maranta makoyana)
BRAIN PLANT
CATHEDRAL WINDOWS
PEACOCK PLANT

Oval-shaped, paper-thin leaves are carried on petioles that may be as much as 60cm (2ft) long, and are intricately patterned. The peacock plant is of a delicate nature; it will rapidly succumb if the temperature is not to its liking. And it must at no time be exposed to direct sunlight, or shrivelling of the leaves will occur.

Small plants are seldom offered for sale. It is usual for the specialist grower to raise plants in very warm beds of peat in the greenhouse; when plants are well established they are potted up into 18cm (7in) pots. For all potting operations a very peaty and open mixture containing some coarse leaf mould will be essential. And following potting it will be necessary to ensure that the soil remains just moist, but never becomes saturated for long periods.

Pests are seldom a problem, but established plants have to be fed with weak liquid fertilizer weekly from spring to autumn.

Take care
Protect from direct sunlight.

- Shade
- Temp: 18-24°C (65-75°F)
- Keep moist and fed

DIFFICULT

Calathea picturata

Oval-shaped leaves some 15cm (6in) long are carried on short petioles that are closely grouped at soil level, producing a plant of neat and compact appearance. The margin of each leaf is green and the centre is a striking silver-grey in colour; the reverse is maroon. As with all calatheas, bright direct sunlight will quickly kill them as leaves begin to shrivel up. Calatheas are happier growing in the shade of bolder plants such as the more spreading types of philodendron, such as *P. bipinnatifidum*.

Cold draughts – and cold conditions generally – must be avoided, and if possible one should provide a moist atmosphere around the plant; this is often best achieved by placing plants in a container that includes a selection of other plants. Large containers are now freely available for making plant arrangements in. Fill a container with moist peat into which the plant pot is plunged to its rim.

Take care
Keep moist and warm.

- ☐ Shade
- ☐ Temp: 18-24°C (65-75°F)
- ☐ Keep moist

Calathea

Left: The silver-grey and green leaves of the Calathea picturata flourish under the protection of taller plants; their exquisite colouring is dependent on shade and very warm temperatures.

Above: The leaves of Calathea zebrina have a velvety texture and bold pattern. They are among the most beautiful of all foliage plants. Warmth and shade are essential conditions.

Calathea zebrina
ZEBRA PLANT

This incredibly beautiful foliage plant will test the skills of anyone. The bold leaves are a deep velvety green with prominent patches of deeper colouring. Maximum height of around 90cm (3ft) may be attained in a well-heated greenhouse where plants are tended with professional care.

It will be fatal to allow this plant to stand in a position exposed to full sunlight for even the shortest space of time. It is remarkable that this plant with its highly coloured exotic appearance should produce such beautiful leaves while growing in shaded locations. But *C. zebrina* always does very much better when placed under and in the shade of taller plants such as ficus and philodendrons, which offer a dark canopy of leaves. When watering, use tepid water and be sure that the soil is thoroughly soaked each time; but allow a drying-out period between waterings. Feed while new leaves are growing.

Take care
Avoid draughts and direct sun.

- ☐ Shade
- ☐ Temp: 18-24°C (65-75°F)
- ☐ Keep moist and fed

DIFFICULT

Codiaeum hybrids
CROTON
JOSEPH'S COAT
VARIEGATED LAUREL

As the common name 'Joseph's coat' suggests, these plants are among the most colourful of all foliage plants.

Full light, with protection from the strongest sunlight, is essential if plants are to retain their bright colouring. In poor light, new growth becomes thin and poor, and colouring is less brilliant. Besides light there is a need for reasonable temperature, without which shedding of lower leaves will be inevitable. Healthy plants that are producing new leaves will require to be kept moist with regular watering, but it is important that the soil should be well drained. Frequent feeding is necessary, though less is needed in winter. On account of vigorous top growth, there will be a mass of roots in the pots of healthy plants. Large plants that seem out of proportion to their pots should be inspected in spring and summer. If well rooted they should be potted into larger pots using loam-based compost.

Take care
Check regularly for red spider.

- Good light
- Temp: 16-21°C (60-70°F)
- Feed and water well

Cyperus

Left: Codiaeum hybrids are among the most highly coloured plants, but must have ample light if they are not to revert to green.

Above: The leaves of Cyperus alternifolius occur at the base of stately stems from which sprout umbrella-like canopies.

Cyperus alternifolius
UMBRELLA PALM
UMBRELLA PLANT
UMBRELLA SEDGE

Of the two cyperus species occasionally offered for sale, this one is the less suitable for indoor conditions on account of its height and its need for very high humidity. The narrow green leaves have little attraction, but green flowers produced on stems that may attain 1.8-2.4m (6-8ft) have a certain fascination. The tall stems of *C. alternifolius* provide an interesting feature at higher level when planting indoor water gardens.

When grown indoors these water-loving plants must be given all the water they require. Although it would be death to most houseplants, place the pot in a large saucer capable of holding a reasonable amount of water, and ensure that the water level is regularly topped up.

Established plants may benefit from regular feeding in liquid or tablet form. Tablets pressed into the soil at the frequency recommended by the manufacturer will provide a continual source of nutrient and is one of the best methods of feeding.

Take care
Keep permanently wet.

☐ Light shade
☐ Temp: 13-18°C (55-65°F)
☐ Wet conditions

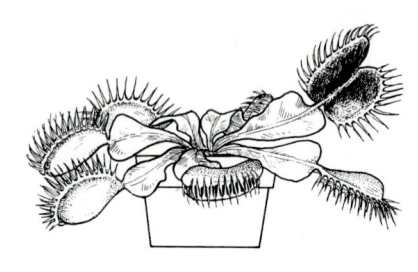

DIFFICULT

Dionaea muscipula
VENUS'S FLYTRAP

The Venus's flytrap is one of the most difficult of potted plants to care for indoors, but the appealing common name will ensure that it retains continued popularity.

Plants may be bought in pots in dormant stage or be acquired in leaf and growing in small pots covered by a plastic dome. The dome offers the plant some protection and helps to retain essential humidity around the plant while it is in transit, so making the dome-covered plant a much better buy. When caring for these plants adequate warmth and high humidity are essential.

When the leaves are touched, a mechanism within the plant induces the oval-shaped leaves to fold together. There are also long stiff hairs along the margins of the leaves; a fly, alighting on the leaf, will activate the mechanism and become trapped. The plant can digest the fly, and feeding flies and minute pieces of meat to the leaves is one way of nourishing the plant.

Take care
Humidity and warmth are essential.

- Light shade
- Temp: 18-27°C (65-80°F)
- Moist atmosphere

Right: The dark green colouring of Fittonia argyroneura nana is heavily veined with a tracery of silvery-grey that gives the oval leaves an attractive appearance. These plants have a creeping habit and need warmth and moisture.

Fittonia

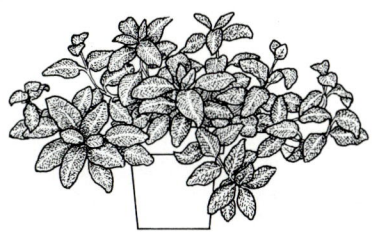

Fittonia argyroneura nana
LITTLE SNAKESKIN PLANT
MOSAIC PLANT
NERVE PLANT
SILVER-NET PLANT

The smaller-leaved version of the silver snakeskin plant is much less demanding than its big brother. The leaves are oval in shape and produced in great quantity by healthy plants. Neat growth and prostrate habit makes them ideal for growing in bottle gardens or disused fish tanks.

Cuttings root with little difficulty in warm, moist and shaded conditions. Several cuttings should go into small pots filled with peaty mixture, and it is often better to overwinter these small plants rather than try to persevere with larger plants. At all stages of potting on a peaty mixture will be essential, and it is better to use shallow containers that will suit the plant's prostrate growth.

Not much troubled by pests; the worst enemy by far is low temperature allied to wet root conditions. Recommended temperature levels must be maintained, and this is especially important during cold weather.

Take care
Avoid wet and cold combination.

- Shade
- Temp: 18-24°C (65-75°F)
- Keep moist and humid

Left: Dionaea muscipula is the well-known Venus's flytrap. Difficult to care for, it has the fascinating ability to catch flies in its sensitive leaves.

DIFFICULT

Above: The paper-thin leaves of Fittonia verschaffeltii are heavily veined with red, resulting in a plant of exotic appearance. Provide warmth, moisture and shade.

Fittonia (large-leaved)
MOSAIC PLANT
NERVE PLANT
SILVER-NET PLANT
SNAKESKIN PLANT

There are two of these that one will be likely to come across, neither of them very easy to care for. With large reddish-green leaves there is *F. verschaffeltii*, and with attractively veined silver leaves there is *F. argyroneura*. Both are of prostrate habit, with leaves tending to curl downwards over their containers. In my experience these plants rarely do well on the windowsill. They fare much better in miniature greenhouses, disused fish tanks or bottle gardens. In such situations the plants are free of draughts.

Bright sunlight will play havoc with the tender foliage so these plants must be in the shade, but not necessarily in very dark locations. When applying water it is best to warm it slightly and to dampen the area surrounding the pot as well as the soil in which the plants are growing. Frequent but small feeds will be better than occasional heavy doses – a little with each watering.

Take care
Avoid low temperatures.

- Shade
- Temp: 18-24°C (65-75°F)
- Keep moist and humid

Below: Microcoelum weddelianum is a slow growing foliage houseplant that will seldom outgrow its allotted space. With age, a basal trunk will form.

Microcoelum weddelianum
(Cocos weddelianum)
WEDDELL PALM

Possibly the most beautiful and delicate of all the many palms offered for sale. However, being slow growing it is seen less often these days, as the commercial grower concentrates his efforts on palms that attain saleable size in a shorter time. One choice specimen of *M. weddelianum* is over 60 years old, with many fine stems reaching a height of some 3m (10ft).

A position out of direct sunlight is advised but one should not put the plant in the darkest corner, as reasonable light is essential to its well-being. Established plants can be fed at every watering with weak liquid fertilizer, with less being given – perhaps none at all – in winter. Some chemicals are harmful, so one should check suitability with the supplier before applying.

Its principal enemy is red spider mite. These mites cause pale discolouration of the foliage and are mostly found on the undersides of leaves.

Take care
Check regularly for red spider.

- Light shade
- Temp: 16-21°C (60-70°F)
- Keep moist and fed

DIFFICULT

Nephthytis podophyllum 'Emerald Gem'
ARROWHEAD VINE
GOOSE FOOT PLANT
PITCHER PLANT

Also offered as *Syngonium podophyllum* 'Emerald Gem', this is one of the easiest of the challenging aroid plants to care for indoors. In bright sunlight the plant will quickly deteriorate, but given moist, warm and shaded conditions it should be trouble-free.

It is an adaptable plant that may be grown as a trailing subject or encouraged to climb by offering some form of support. Being an aroid it will develop natural aerial roots along the main stem. It will assist the plant if the supporting stake can be covered with a layer of moss; the moss should be bound lightly to the support with non-corrosive plastic-covered wire, and kept moist. These plants also do well when grown by water culture. Although moisture at their roots and in the surrounding atmosphere is important, exercise care when watering, and ensure that the soil dries out a little between waterings, particularly during the winter. Feed regularly except in winter.

Take care
Keep moist, warm and shaded.

- Light shade
- Temp: 16-21°C (60-70°F)
- Keep moist

Above: Nephthytis podophyllum 'Emerald Gem' thrives in shade and humidity but will rapidly deteriorate if given too much sun.

Below: Nephthytis podophyllum 'White Butterfly' is a free-growing plant of the Araceae family, needing moisture and shade. This plant will climb or trail.

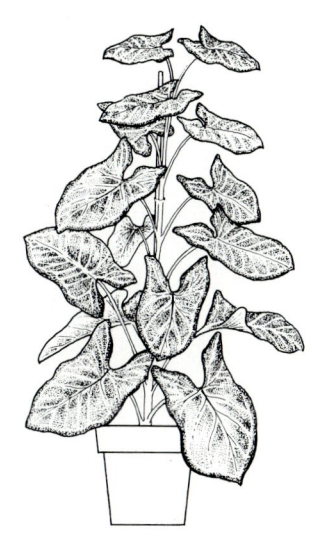

Nephthytis

Nephthytis podophyllum 'White Butterfly'
ARROWHEAD VINE
GOOSE FOOT PLANT
PITCHER PLANT

Also known as *Syngonium podophyllum* 'White Butterfly'; the common name of goose foot relates to the shape of the adult leaf. Pale green leaves are suffused with white, and the plant will trail or climb as required.

It will have to be kept moist at all times, with occasional misting of the foliage with tepid water. The goose foot has adapted amazingly well to hydroculture, the technique of growing plants in water with nutrient solution added. In this instance the plant has all the soil washed away from its roots before it is converted to water culture. The roots are then suspended in clay granules (a sort of artificial pebble), and a special nutrient is added to the water for the plant to feed on. If the simple directions concerning watering and feeding are followed, the goose foot will grow at three times the rate of the same plant in soil, and frequent pruning is needed.

Take care
Avoid dry conditions.

- Light shade
- Temp: 16-21°C (60-70°F)
- Keep moist and fed

DIFFICULT

Above: With dark green markings on a silvery-grey background and naturally shiny leaves, Peperomia argyreia is one of the most attractive in this genus.

Peperomia argyreia
RADIATOR PLANT
RUGBY FOOTBALL PLANT
WATERMELON BEGONIA
WATERMELON PEPEROMIA

Sadly, this is one of the older houseplants that is not seen so frequently these days. The leaves are an interesting grey-green colour with darker stripes that radiate from the centre of the leaf. The darker stripes give the plant its name of Rugby football plant.

These compact plants should be grown in shallow pans of soilless potting mixture, with protection from direct sunlight. Watering should be done with care; err on the side of dry rather than wet conditions. Established plants can be given weak liquid fertilizer with every watering from early spring to late summer, but none in winter. Sound leaves can be removed and cut into quarters that are placed in upright position in pure peat in warm conditions. The quartered leaf will produce roots and eventually leaves along the length of the cut edge below soil level. During propagation, ensure that the cuttings do not become too wet.

Take care
Avoid winter wetness and cold.

☐ Light shade
☐ Temp: 13-18°C (55-65°F)
☐ Keep moist and fed

Piper

Piper ornatum
CELEBESE PEPPER
ORNAMENTAL PEPPER

The waxy leaves are 7.5-10cm (3-4in) long, deep green in colour and beautifully marked in silvery pink. For the best effect, provide plants with a light framework onto which they can be trained.

Warmth is essential, and the air around the plant must not become too dry; spray leaves with tepid water from a hand mister. When potting on, avoid large pots; these plants prefer pots in proportion to the top growth. Soilless potting mixture suits them best, but it will be important to ensure that the plant is fed regularly (not in winter) and that soil never becomes too dry. Very wet conditions will be equally harmful, so allow some drying out between waterings. Plants lose much of their colouring if grown in dark corners. Provide good light but avoid direct sunlight.

Firm leaves with a piece of stem attached can be rooted in peat in warm conditions during spring in a propagating case.

Take care
Avoid winter cold and wetness.

- Good light
- Temp: 18-24°C (65-75°F)
- Keep moist

DIFFICULT

Above: The anchor fronds of Platycerium bifurcatum are to position the plant; the main fronds resemble stag's antlers.

Platycerium bifurcatum
STAG'S HORN FERN

Essential requirements of all platyceriums are moist, warm and shaded conditions, and if one cannot offer all three of those then it will be difficult to grow these plants.

Schefflera

Plants are normally grown in pots filled with peat mixture and will seldom do well in anything that is too heavy and root-restricting. But besides the conventional pot they may be grown as mobiles, or for hanging on a wall. The plant is removed from its pot and the roots are wrapped in fresh sphagnum moss before the complete bundle is firmly secured to its support: plastic-covered wire is useful for this purpose. The plant can then be soaked thoroughly in a bucket of water and allowed to drain before it is put in position. Subsequent watering should follow the same lines.

Scale insects attaching themselves to all parts of the plant are by far the worst pest, and should be wiped off with a firm sponge that has been soaked in insecticide.

Take care
Avoid excessive drying out.

- Shade
- Temp: 16-21°C (60-70°F)
- Keep moist

Below: Schefflera arboricola are upright, green-foliaged plants with palmate leaves that offer a canopy of umbrella-like growth.

Schefflera arboricola
PARASOL PLANT
STARLEAF
UMBRELLA TREE

In some parts of the world this plant may be seen labelled as *Heptapleurum* which it strongly resembles.

However, the difference lies in the size of the leaves. Both are green and palmate, but the heptapleurum leaf is very much larger.

The parasol plant has an alarming habit of shedding leaves for no apparent reason. My view is that they often get much colder than the temperature recommended here. If plants are very wet at their roots and are subjected to low temperatures as well they will almost certainly lose leaves. There is some compensation, however, in that plants produce fresh growth later if the conditions improve.

Individual stems will grow to a height of 3m (10ft) in a comparatively short time. However, one can cut the stem back to more manageable size at any time of the year. As a result of this pruning treatment the plant will produce many more side growths.

Take care
Avoid winter wetness and cold.

- Good light, no strong sun
- Temp: 16-21°C (60-70°F)
- Keep moist and fed

DIFFICULT

Schefflera arboricola variegata
VARIEGATED PARASOL PLANT
VARIEGATED UMBRELLA TREE

The fingered leaves and habit of growth are exactly the same as the green form, but the leaves are liberally splashed with vivid yellow colouring to give the plant a glowing brightness when it is placed among others in a large display. Elegance lies in the graceful and light distribution of leaves and stems, which enables one to see through and beyond to other plants in the display. And indoors it is equally important to have graceful plants rather than a solid wall of foliage.

In common with almost all the variegated plants this one should have a light location, but exposure to bright sun close to window-panes should be avoided if the leaves are not to be scorched. This is especially important if the leaves have been treated with chemicals. Most of the leaf-cleaning chemicals are perfectly suitable for the majority of plants, but one should never expose treated plants to direct sunlight.

Take care
Avoid winter wetness and cold.

- Good light, no strong sun
- Temp: 16-21°C (60-70°F)
- Keep moist and fed

Top right: Schefflera arboricola variegata has the same habit as the green form, but is slower growing. It is mostly yellow.

Scindapsus

Scindapsus aureus 'Marble Queen'
(Epipremnum pinnatum)
GOLDEN POTHOS
VARIEGATED DEVIL'S IVY

The white variegated devil's ivy will test the skill of the most accomplished grower. Most plants with a large area of white are a problem, and this is no exception.

A temperature over 18°C (65°F) is needed, particularly in winter. Also, it will be necessary to create a humid atmosphere around the plant. (This should not be confused with watering the plant to excess.) The simplest way is to provide a large saucer or tray filled with pebbles on which the plant can stand; the saucer can be partly filled with water, but the level should never be above the surface of the pebbles, as it is important that the plant pot should not stand in water. In a warm room such a saucer will continually give off moisture around the plant. Moist peat surrounding the plant pot is another way of providing moisture; and there are numerous types of troughs with capillary matting for placing plants on.

Take care
Keep moist and warm.

- Light shade
- Temp: 18-24°C (65-75°F)
- Keep moist and fed

Left: Humidity and warmth are necessary to cultivate the white variegated Scindapsus aureus 'Marble Queen'.

DIFFICULT

Sonerila margaritacea
FROSTED SONERILA

A neat and colourful plant, with prominent silver markings on the upper surface of leaves, and purple underneath. They are extremely difficult to manage if treated simply as a potted plant for the windowsill.

Low temperatures, draughts, full sun and overwatering all make life difficult for the tender sonerila. Sonerila demands even temperature and even amount of moisture above all. A glass case or bottle garden offers draught-free conditions that can also be maintained at an evenly moist level much more easily than can be done if plants are simply placed on a windowsill among cold draughts and fluctuating temperatures.

Use tepid rain water, not water drawn direct from the tap. Feed regularly with weak liquid fertilizer while plants are producing new leaves; when potting, they will do best in soilless mixture. Ensure that soilless mixtures do not become excessively wet or dry.

Take care
Avoid cold and wetness in winter.

- Light shade
- Temp: 18-24°C (65-75°F)
- Keep moist

Stromanthe

Stromanthe amabilis

This plant belongs to the same family as the calatheas and marantas. The oval-shaped leaves come to a point and are a bluish green in colour with bands of stronger colour running the length of the leaf. They overlap one another and are produced at soil level from a creeping rhizome. They reach a length of about 15-23cm (6-9in) and a width of 5cm (2in).

New plants are easily raised by dividing existing clumps into smaller sections and potting them up as individuals. The soil for this ought to be a good houseplant mixture containing a reasonable quantity of peat. Being squat plants they will also be better suited to shallow pans rather than full-depth pots. Shade is essential, as plants simply shrivel up when subjected to strong sunlight for any length of time. Soil should be kept moist, but it is absolutely necessary to ensure that it is moistness that is the aim and not total saturation.

Take care
Maintain warmth and humidity.

- Shade
- Temp: 18-24°C (65-75°F)
- Keep moist

Below: Similar in appearance to some of the marantas, Stromanthe amabilis forms neat low mounds of growth but needs careful culture to succeed. Warm, humid conditions suit it best.

INDEX

Above: The polka dot plant (Hypoestes sanguinolenta) forms a beautiful picture of delicate, pink-mottled leaves. Untidy plants can easily be pruned and the trimmings used as cuttings.

Index

Abutilon hybridum 'Sevitzia' 14-15
Abutilon sevitzia 14-15
Acclimatizing new plants 7
Aglaonema crispum 'Silver Queen' 31
Aglaonema pseudobracteatum 31
Alocasia indica 70-71
Aluminium plant 23
Ananas bracteatus striatus 32
Angel's wings 75
Anthurium crystallinum 72
Aphids 13
Aralia elegantissima 46
Arrowhead vine 84-85
Asplenium nidus 72-73

Balfour aralia 67
Beaucarnea recurvata 33
Beefsteak plant 19
Begonia masoniana 16
Begonia rex 14, 17
Begonia vine 37
Benjamin tree 50
Bird's nest fern 72-73
Blood leaf 19
Blushing bromeliad 60-61
Botrytis 13
Bottle ponytail 33
Boundary plant 14, 28-29
Bowstring hemp 26
Brain plant 74-75
Buffalo grass 28
Burro's tail 69
Buying, advice on 6-7

Caladium hybrids 75
Calathea makoyana 6, 74-75
Calathea picturata 76
Calathea zebrina 77
Canary date palm 65
Canary Island date 65
Cartwheel plant 60-61
Cathedral windows 74-75
Celebese pepper 87
Ceropegia woodii 34-35
Chamaedorea elegans 36
Chicken gizzard 19
Chinese evergreen 31
Chinese lantern 14-15
Cissus discolor 37
Climbing begonia 37
Cocos weddelianum 83
Columnea banksii variegata 38
Compost, advice on 9
Cordyline terminalis 'Firebrand' 39
Cryptanthus bromeliodes 'It' 40
Cryptanthus bromeliodes tricolor 41
Cryptanthus 'Foster's Favourite' 42
Crystal anthurium 72
Cut-leaf philodendron 59
Cyperus alternifolius 79

Dagger plant 28-29
Devil's tongue 26
Dieffenbachia amoena 42-43
Dieffenbachia amoena 'Tropic Snow' 42-43
Dieffenbachia maculata 44
Dieffenbachia maculata 'Exotica' 45

Dinner plate aralia 67
Dionaea muscipula 6, 80
Disease, advice on 13
Display, advice on 10-12
Dizygotheca elegantissima 46
Donkey's tail 69
Dracaena deremensis 46-47
Dracaena deremensis 'Bausei' 46-47
Dracaena deremensis 'Souvenir de Schriever' 46-47
Dracaena fragrans 48
Dracaena fragrans 'Massangeana' 48
Dracaena fragrans 'Victoria' 48
Dracaena marginata tricolor 49
Dracaena reflexa variegata 24
Dumb cane 42-45

Earth star 40-42
Elephant foot 33
Elephant's ear 22, 71, 75
Epipremnum pinnatum 91

False aralia 46
Feather palm 65, 66
Feeding, advice on 8
Ficus benjamina 50
Ficus benjamina 'Hawaii' 51
Ficus elastica 'Europa' 52-53
Ficus lyrata 53
Fiddle leaf fig 53
Fiddleleaf philodendron 64
Fittonia argyroneura nana 81
Fittonia (large-leaved) 82-83
Flaming dragon tree 39
Flamingo plant 56
Flowering maple 14-15
Freckle face 56
Frosted sonerila 92
Fruit salad plant 59

Golden bird's nest 68
Golden evergreen 31
Golden pothos 91
Good-luck palm 36
Good-luck plant 26
Goose foot plant 84-85
Grevillea robusta 18
Grooming, advice on 9
Gynura sarmentosa 54

Hearts entangled 34-35
Hearts on a string 34-35
Herringbone plant 57
Horsehead philodendron 64
Horse's tail 69
Howeia forsteriana 55
Humble plant 20-21
Hypoestes sanguinolenta 56, 94

Iresine herbstii 19
Iron cross begonia 16
Ivory pineapple 32
Ivy-leaf peperomia 63

Java fig 50

Kentia forsteriana 55
Kentia palm 55

INDEX

Lamb's tail 69
Little snakeskin plant 81
Live-and-die 20-21

Maranta leuconeura erythrophylla 57
Maranta leuconeura kerchoviana 58
Maranta makoyana 74-75
Mealy bug 13
Measles plant 56
Mexican breadfruit 59
Microcoelum weddelianum 83
Mimosa pudica 20-21
Miniature date palm 66
Mist spraying, advice on 8
Monstera deliciosa 6, 59
Mosaic plant 81-83
Mother-in-law's tongue 14, 26, 42-45

Neanthe bella 36
Neoregelia carolinae tricolor 60-61
Nephthytis podophyllum 'Emerald Gem' 84
Nephthytis podophyllum 'White Butterfly' 85
Nerve plant 81-83
Nest fern 72-73

Ornamental pepper 87

Painted leaf begonia 17
Panda plant 64
Pandanus baptiste 62
Paradise palm 55
Parasol plant 89
Parlour palm 36
Peacock plant 6, 75
Pellionia daveauana 21
Peperomia argyreia 86
Peperomia griseoargentea 63
Peperomia hederifolia 63
Pests 13
Philodendron bipinnatifidum 64
Philodendron hastatum 22
Phoenix canariensis 65
Phoenix roebelinii 66
Pilea cadierei nana 23
Pink-dot plant 56
Piper ornatum 87
Pitcher plant 84-85
Platinum peperomia 63
Platycerium bifurcatum 88
Pleomele reflexa variegata 24
Polka dot plant 56, 94
Polyscias balfouriana 67
Polyscias balfouriana 'Pinnochio' 67
Ponytail plant 33
Powdery mildew 13
Prayer plant 57-59
Pteris cretica albo-lineata 25
Purple heart 27
Pygmy date palm 66

Rabbit's-foot 58-59
Rabbit's tracks 58-59
Radiator plant 63, 86
Rainbow-star 40, 41
Red spider mite 13
Rex begonia 14, 17
Roebelin palm 66
Rosary vine 34-35
Rugby football plant 86

St Augustine's grass 28
Sansevieria trifasciata 14

Sansevieria trifasciata 'Golden Hahni' 68
Sansevieria trifasciata 'Laurentii' 26
Scale insects 13
Schefflera arboricola 89
Schefflera arboricola variegata 90
Scindapsus aureus 'Marble Queen' 91
Screw pine 62
Sedum morganianum 69
Setcreasea purpurea 27
Sensitive plant 20-21
Shame plant 20-21
Silk oak 18
Silver-leaf peperomia 63
Silver-net plant 81-83
Silver ripple 63
Silver spear 31
Small-leaved rubber tree 50
Snake plant 26
Snakeskin plant 82-83
Sonerila margaritacea 92
Song of India 24
Sooty mould 13
Spanish bayonet 28-29
Split-leaf philodendron 59
Stag's horn fern 88
Starleaf 89
Stenotaphrum secundatum 28
Strap flower 72
String of hearts 34-35
Striped dracaena 46-47
Stromanthe amabilis 93
Sun scald, advice on 13
Swiss cheese plant 6, 59

Temperature, advice on 8
Thatch-leaf palm 55
Touch-me-not 20-21
Trailing begonia 37
Trailing watermelon begonia 21
Tree philodendron 64
Tuftroot 42-45

Umbrella palm 79
Umbrella plant 79
Umbrella sedge 79
Umbrella tree 89

Variegated Cretan brake 25
Variegated devil's ivy 91
Variegated goldfish plant 38
Variegated Madagascar dragon tree 49
Variegated parasol plant 90
Variegated rubber plant 52-53
Variegated silhouette plant 49
Variegated table fern 25
Variegated umbrella tree 90
Variegated weeping fig 51
Velvet plant 54
Venus's flytrap 6, 80

Watering, advice on 8
Watermelon begonia 86
Watermelon peperomia 86
Watermelon pilea 23
Weddell palm 83
Weeping fig 50
Whitefly 13
Wilting, advice on 13
Window plant 59

Yucca aloifolia 6, 14, 28-29

Zebra plant 77